Carol Schiro (

STRATEGIC NETWORKING

for Introverts, Extroverts, and Everyone in Between

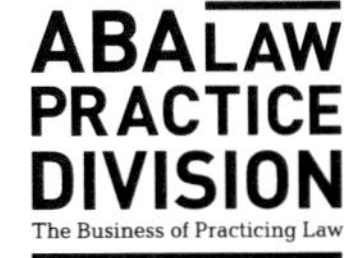

Cover design by Elmarie Jara/ABA Design

Printed in the United States of America.

23 22 21 20 19   5 4 3 2

Library of Congress Cataloging-in-Publication Data

Library of Congress Cataloging-in-Publication Data
Names: Greenwald, Carol S. (Carol Schiro), author.
Title: Strategic networking for introverts, extroverts, and everyone in
between / by Carol Schiro Greenwald.
Description: Chicago : American Bar Association, 2019. | Includes
bibliographical references and index.
Identifiers: LCCN 2018055621 (print) | LCCN 2018060212 (ebook) | ISBN
9781641053785 (epub) | ISBN 9781641053778 (print : alk. paper)
Subjects: LCSH: Social networks. | Introverts.
Classification: LCC HM741 (ebook) | LCC HM741 .G75 2019 (print) | DDC
302.23/1—dc23
LC record available at https://lccn.loc.gov/2018055621

Discounts are available for books ordered in bulk. Special consideration is given to state bars, CLE programs, and other bar-related organizations. Inquire at Book Publishing, ABA Publishing, American Bar Association, 321 N. Clark Street, Chicago, Illinois 60654-7598.

www.ShopABA.org

Reviews

Why is networking important? Because it's the best way to build connections with people who may ultimately turn into clients. This is a must-read book for the introvert and for the extrovert because the author offers something for both: for the introvert, Carol's tips on how to create a plan to network boosts the introvert's confidence so that they can feel more at ease when networking. And for the extrovert, her tips on how to stay focused enough to create a networking plan can elevate the extrovert's networking from just having fun to creating actual networking opportunities. This book reflects not only Carol's networking experience, but that of the 35 people she interviewed in a variety of professions and industries. You can tell Carol is a strategic planner by the way she strategically organized this book to appeal to all types of learners: For instance, for those too busy to read every page of this book, Carol provides chapter summaries at the end of each chapter. For those who like to read text, there's plenty of text, and for those who are visual learners, there's plenty of charts and graphs. For those who like filling in worksheets to guide themselves through a process, there are plenty of worksheets, from the Elevator Speech Components worksheet to the Referral Strategies worksheet, etc. And, for those who want specific networking suggestions, check out Appendix 3, Additional Insights. Go forth and network!

Carole Levitt
Author, *Internet for Lawyers*

Carol has gifted us all a substantial professional favor by creating this phenomenal roadmap for networking and business development. Her ability to create a game plan that includes the most effective strategies for skill development and implementation is abundantly valuable. A quick read with palpable ROI right at our fingertips—thank you, Carol!

Traci Ray
Executive Director, Barran Liebman LLP

In this book you will find a plethora of anecdotes that will be sure to resonate with any reader via one of the many in-depth interviews that Carol conducted from professionals in various industries. Carol does an excellent job of providing clear, concise action steps to help a novice networker get started, but also delivers enough high-level tips for even the most networked professionals to find great value in reading the book.

Jennifer Scalzi
CEO and Founder, Calibrate Legal

Having known Carol Greenwald for over 15 years, I've always turned to her for advice and, frankly, inspiration. While she's helped me in numerous ways, her particular strength is networking. That's why I'm so grateful she has taken the time to gather her thoughts on this subject, yielding a book that's a handy resource I intend to share with my clients.

John Rumely
Advisor, Coach, Business Development Professional

Carol's approach to strategic networking is like being offered a Ph.D. course, when you had only been offered a high school course previously. Her examples are clear, her suggested modeling language powerful, and her real-life stories illustrate the impact of networking well in myriad situations. Whether you are a veteran professional, new lawyer, or professional services provider, this book will enable you to focus on your goals and hone your skills. Simply put, this is the best resource I have ever read about professional networking. I dare you to read it, implement it, and not watch your business grow.

Linda Orton
Chief Marketing Officer & Managing Director, Alvarez & Marsal

Strategic Networking is the right book for the "introvert who networks," for the "hyper-extroverts" and everyone in between who needs guidance on effective networking. Carol incorporates real-life examples from networkers throughout and explains how to network in a way that is best suited to a person's personality. Most useful of all, the book provides a practical approach to building a strategic networking process that will surely yield results.

Despina C. Kartson
Global Director, Business Development & Communications

Strategic Networking isn't just another book on networking. Or worse, networking for people who don't like to networking. It's both a resource-filled, nuts-and-bolts guide and a high-level set of stories on the how and why of networking. Carol does a great job teaching how networking is done with step-by-step directions, as well guides and worksheets that can help the uninitiated and the networking challenged. But she also shows how it can pay off by allowing experts (and schlubs like me) who have built businesses and careers through networking to show the value it's created for them. While there are an increasing number, maybe endless number, of ways to connect and get to know someone today there's still nothing like meeting face to-face and pressing the flesh. And Carol's done you the favor of putting everything you need to know in this great, readable volume. Carol's book should be the starting point for anyone looking to grow their business or career through networking. (Hint - that includes you, because it includes everyone!)

Dan Lear
Chief Instigator, Right Brain Law

Whether you think you're an expert or a novice networker, this book is a must read. It reinforces that good networking is about giving, not taking, and that effective networking is a strategy that can be learned. Carol thoughtfully breaks down the process step by step showing us all not only how to think, but how to take action. And action leads to results. Well done!

Nancy B. Schess, Esq.
Partner, Klein, Zelman, Rothermel, Jacobs & Schess LLP

Strategic Networking is a practical, hands-on, and thorough guide to help anyone expand their reach and visibility for personal and professional success. As it is with most skills, those who network effectively make it look easy. But networking doesn't come naturally to many people. Carol's book provides an excellent roadmap to boost your networking chops, with numerous anecdotes and lessons learned from fellow professionals, handy charts and checklists to get started, and, most compelling to me, tools to help a busy professional weave networking time into a packed schedule in a way that's additive, rather than dilutive. Just as networking is an excellent investment of time, learning from Carol how to effectively network was an excellent investment of my time. I thoroughly enjoyed it.

Timothy B. Corcoran
Management Consultant & Former CEO, BringinTim.com, @tcorcoran

Table of Contents

Introduction

I am not a natural networker; I am an introvert who networks. I work in an industry where, in order to succeed, I need to interact with a wide group of people, some of whom I know well and many I don't know at all. I learned to network successfully by creating a comfortable process for myself. Usually, when I join groups I get involved on committees, often ending up as a member of the board or president. Having a role helps me feel useful and comfortable in the group. If you ever see me at a large group function, probably I am one of the speakers. Again, a role that keeps me grounded and calm.

I've made a good living coaching lawyers and other professionals in practical skills, including leadership, management, business development, and networking. Being an intellectual introvert has helped me communicate with other intellectual introverts. I share the lessons I've learned. I teach my clients how to research and plan, how to create "safe havens" from which to venture forth and explain the why of what they do. Practicing what I preach has enabled me to participate in many wonderful group encounters, lead important and interesting organizations and projects, and keep my own company's pipeline filled with stimulating, remunerative work.

I wrote this book for all the "nonnaturals" in the world who are afraid of the networking process. The book offers anyone who takes the time to read it the tools to turn ad hoc networking into a series of planned strategic steps that will move them toward their goals. The security of a plan and preparation offers introverts the confidence they need to venture forth. The book is also for all the hyper-extroverts who sail through an event having too much fun to maximize the available networking opportunities. Strategic networking keeps extroverts focused; helps introverts feel safe; and encourages everyone to make efficient, effective use of their networking time.

Because I am not a networking natural, I enlisted the help of 35 friends and colleagues who are effective networkers. All of those interviewed are listed in Appendix 1. Between March 2017 and January 2018, I conducted one- to two-hour in-person interviews with each individual, asking him/her to explain the "why and how" of his/her networking activities. Their answers appear throughout the book, offering real-life, from-the-trenches experiences in the strategic networking process outlined in these 12 chapters.

The group includes attorneys (some of whom no longer practice law and have gone on to other pursuits), finance professionals, and a dozen people in other businesses. About half are women; half are men. They range in age from mid-thirties to mid-sixties. Most of them live and work in the Northeast. Three make their living running networking groups, and 11 founded one or more networking groups, many of which are discussed in the book.

Behind every book is a village. My thanks go to so many people who helped me. Andrew Elowitt, my American Bar Association Law Practice Division colleague, liked my idea and helped me get it approved by the Law Practice Division publishing board. He also joined the editing team and, with them, improved the text immeasurably. My thanks to John Rumely, my friend and colleague from my professional community, chosen by me to validate the usefulness of the book for the legal marketing community. John was also a careful reader of the original text.

The team from Lachina, the professional firm that publishes ABA Law Practice Division books, led by Molly Montanaro, has been supportive and helpful throughout the process. And, last but not least, my thanks to two important lawyers in my life who took the time to help me. My brother, Richard B. Schiro, a Texas litigator, read every word even though "networking is not his thing" and found all the padded paragraphs, clichés, grammatical errors, redundant words, and mixed-up thoughts. My friend and colleague, Donna Drumm, found time in a crazy schedule to make sense of and improve the text in very redlined chapters so I could get my edits in on time. To both of them my thanks for making the book more readable.

Thanks also to my friends and family, especially Richard Zuckerman, for supporting me in this endeavor.

Any errors in the content are obviously all my own.

C.

Strategic Networking Explained 1

Networking is more than a marketing technique. It is a way to build your service or business by engaging in activities that are natural to humans. We are mentally programmed to connect with other people, help them thrive, and, in helping others, flourish as well. The best networkers create these positive associations. They want to understand the needs of others and help them move forward. As they gain reputations for helping others succeed, they too grow.

This kind of networking is positive. It creates affirmative feelings of support, understanding, and trust between the giver and the given. It is strategic because it is goal driven. In this book we look at the why, what, and how of networking:

- Why it is possible to do well by doing good.
- What strategic networking is.
- How to proceed in the most effective way.

On the one hand, data show "that more than 80 percent of professionals consider networking to be crucial to their success."[1] On the other hand, data show that "one in four don't network at all."[2] This book is for people in both camps: those who know they should but don't, and those who do but not as successfully as they would like.

To get a clearer sense of how master networkers approach networking, I interviewed 35 of them from a variety of industries and professions. When you

1. Email invitation from Network After Work—Seattle, April 16, 2018, info@networkafterwork.com.

2. Aja Frost, "15 Surprising Stats on Networking and Face-To-Face Communication," updated November 15, 2017, https://blog.hubspot.com/sales/face-to-face-networking-stats.

ask these networking pros to explain why networking is important to them, the same concepts recur over and over. They emphasize the feel-good aspects:

- Meeting people, interesting people, people with similar values and interests
- Building relationships
- Helping others and, in turn, being helped by others
- Expanding their horizons
- Being a connector
- Being visible to those who are important to them
- Becoming part of a community
- Following conversations of interest
- Sharing their expertise

For these professionals, effective networking is an important component of their success. Their investments in networking activities have enabled them to become rainmakers, build successful relationships, and enjoy reputations as effective connectors.

David Maister, a prominent law practice pioneer and consultant to professionals, wrote that to be successful in life one should "spend your investment time as seriously as income time. . . . If your investment time is spent wisely on carefully chosen activities, you will have the ability to significantly affect your future success—and lifestyle."[3]

Sidebar 1.1 A Tale of Two Taylors

Once upon a time two Taylors went to a networking event. Taylor Together, a corporate lawyer, looks forward to networking because s/he enjoys meeting new people, reconnecting with old friends, making introductions, and deepening relationships that often lead to new business. Taylor Together considers networking activities a necessary and pleasurable part of the work day. S/he has built a business through networking, living by the mantra that "what goes around, comes around."[4] As s/he listens to other people, Taylor is always thinking about how s/he can help them attain their goals.

Taylor Timid, also a business lawyer, puts networking in the same category as an hour at the dentist. S/he resents the interruption in an already overflowing busy day. Taylor Timid only networks because everyone tells him/her that "networking is a precondition for business growth. If you are not visible, you won't be found." Taylor typically speeds through gatherings, asking about others but not staying around to listen to their replies. S/he rarely follows up or follows through on conversations.

3. David H. Maister, *True Professionalism* (Simon & Schuster, 1997), p. 48.
4. Gotham City Networking Group's mantra.

Both Taylors attend the same Attain Success Group cocktail party.

- *Taylor Together arrives early to work the room. S/he has done some research about the event and attendees and has a mental list of people to meet, those s/he wants to reconnect with and what s/he might add to conversations. Taylor Together looks attractively professional and is obviously in an outgoing, good mood as reflected in her/his body language.*
- *Taylor Timid enters late, grabs a cup of coffee, and exchanges cards with some people in the coffee line. S/he looks disheveled, grumpy and a bit out of sorts. Taylor sits down at a table and pulls out her/his phone to check for any messages. A few people drifting by say hello. Taylor Timid wonders why s/he decided to attend this meeting in the first place.*

Back in the office, Taylor Together spends 15 minutes updating his/her contact list and making plans to keep in touch with two people s/he met who could, over time, become clients. S/he thought to her/himself, what a useful, engaging event. Taylor Timid leaves feeling s/he has wasted an evening on a boring event with uninteresting people of no particular value to her/his practice. S/he takes 15 business cards out of a jacket pocket and throws them in the circular file.

The moral of this tale is that networking is what you make it. With some preparation and a forward-thinking attitude about the event, Taylor Together's evening led to two new connections and interesting conversations. Taylor Timid had a handful of business cards from strangers to add to her/his email list. When networking is an ad hoc, thrown-together, last-minute activity, as it was for Taylor Timid, it is rarely worth more than the effort put into it.

Now, let's look at how it plays out in real life by sketching the activities of two women, one a lawyer and the other a financial planner, both of whom build businesses, resources, and friendships through strategic networking.

Abby Rosmarin, Lawyer, Mediator, Mental Health Counselor

Abby Rosmarin is a lawyer, mediator, conflict coach, NYS Licensed Mental Health Counselor, and executive director of the New York Association of Collaborative Professionals. She thinks of the word "networking" as negative because in her mind it is linked to "aggressive salesmanship." Yet, she is an experienced, effective networker who has built her practice through networking. She networks to learn, to mentor, and to help others. For her, "networking is about learning from colleagues, sharing common interests and seeking opportunities for experiences with like-minded people." She doesn't believe in speed networking, business card exchanges, or one-minute intros.

Abby thinks that typical networking activities elicit surface knowledge of other people. She wants an in-depth interpersonal connection so that she feels she really knows which individual in her network can best help each client. Abby broadens her network by using social media to connect to people she reads about, and then typically arranges to meet them in person to get to know the actual person. Her LinkedIn groups similarly reflect the therapist lens through which she defines meaningful relationships.

Her networking is guided by her interests and beliefs. She follows her inclinations—she has studied a range of topics from other fields, such as medical bioethics, to enhance her interdisciplinary collaboration with others and expand her ability to help her clients. Her list of current organization memberships—legal, social services, and community services—reflects this approach. [See her current memberships in Appendix 3, pages 207–209.]

Abby and two friends founded WESTCHESTER PROFESSIONALS: Face-to-Face in 2013 and disbanded it in its present form on April 30, 2018. The impetus for the group was Abby's interest in getting to know other professionals well enough to trust them as resources for her clients. Their goals were spelled out in the group's mission statement.

Face-to-Face Mission Statement

WESTCHESTER PROFESSIONALS: Face-to-Face is a multi-disciplinary networking group founded on the belief that we serve our clients and our professions most effectively when we develop collaborative relationships with people in our network.

As our name indicates, we meet face-to-face in a setting that encourages participants to challenge beliefs, expand horizons, and look beyond business card credentials as we build a network that is integrated and collaborative.

Our meetings are didactic presentations, small and large group discussions as well as experiential projects. All these focus on the practical and interpersonal aspects of building connections, which is the foundation of our organization.[5]

Face to Face Members

Our members are professionals who are engaged in services with the common thread of guiding clients through changes that lead to an improved quality of life.

5. On WESTCHESTER PROFESSIONALS: Face-to-Face meeting notices.

> We represent a cross section of helping professions—including but not limited to psychotherapists, family laws attorneys, physical and spiritual healers, organizers, coaches.

The group[6] typically met quarterly in Abby's home for breakfast and "structured conversations," which the three founders designed before the meeting. The focus was on learning. Each meeting had a theme that was introduced by a question people had to answer when they gave their introduction to the group. For example,

- Say your name and tell us what your shoes say about you.
- What does belonging to a group mean?
- Tell two truths and a lie about yourself.
- If you could create a bumper sticker that gives a window into who you are, what would it be?

After introductions, the leaders teed up the meeting topic in more detail and the group as a whole discussed it, or they talked first in smaller clusters before sharing insights as a group.

The purpose of these exercises was to jointly experience the discussion in the safety of the group. Discussions concluded with members sharing what the conversation meant for each of them. Members felt the personal nature of the discussions enabled them to know each other as "whole persons," creating a level of intimacy and community that gave rise to trusted relationships.

The group as it existed for five years has been disbanded, but Abby hopes it will evolve into something else. At the last meeting Abby said, "I don't see this as an end because we all know each other. I look forward to what happens next." Isabel, one of the three cofounders, promised to set up a meeting to discuss the next iteration of the group.

The group embodied Abby's networking precepts. With or without it, her networking continues to reflect her own interest in and enthusiasm for knowing other people in a deeply personal way, sharing new ideas, and contributing to social progress.

Stacy Francis, President and CEO, Francis Financial

Stacy Francis, a financial planner and wealth management advisor, started her company, Francis Financial, in 2002. She networks in order to help as many people as she can and grow her business.

6. Information from Personal Interview, August 7, 2017, and Greenwald attendance at two meetings in 2018.

Stacy believes that networking is an essential component of success. She says,

"I adore helping people. Networking has been the key to my success. I liken networking to a garden. In the beginning there is a lot of hard work. But you learn from experience and experimenting. It takes time to grow. And then you reap the harvest.

Without networking I wouldn't have been able to grow my company and add colleagues who share the work with me so I can spend quality time with my family. Networking is the engine of growth.

I think if you are not networking you are doomed to fail. If you are afraid to do it, your definition is wrong."

How did she do it?

She began by joining groups that would help her learn how to network effectively and also teach her marketing skills. As she became more proficient she began building personal networking groups strategically crafted to move her toward her goals. [See Stacy's current group memberships in Appendix 3, page 209.]

For example, 13 years ago, she started a general-purpose group, Allied Professional Women [APW], an open networking group that met monthly to share ideas about growing businesses and to showcase the diverse businesses in the group. For Stacy it was a way to learn, build resources in allied fields, and link with referral partners. She was the spark plug that gave the group direction and cohesion. She "created a community of incredible women who were able to collaborate together and really support one another."[7] Her group mailing list grew from a handful to over 600 women.

Then, in November 2017, she made the decision to shut it down because her strategy became more focused. She moved from an emphasis on all women in financial difficulties to a niche market: divorced and widowed women. She wanted to devote more time to groups focused on this niche market as opposed to the eclectic assortment of businesses in the APW group.

So, in 2017, she turned her attention to growing the NY chapter of the Association of Divorce Financial Planners [ADFP], an organization which she has been the Chapter Director of since 2011. For Stacy, it provides information and access to other professionals in her field, many of whom have become friends, colleagues, and referral partners.

7. Stacy Francis email to members of the APW group, November 16, 2017.

ADFP members are divorce financial planning practitioners (both men and women) that use the divorce financial planning process as defined by ADFP. They must charge a reasonable fee-for-service and cannot be compensated in other ways for providing divorce financial planning services. To be accepted as a member, applicants must provide evidence supporting satisfaction of certain educational, experience, and ethical criteria. Divorce financial planners can explain financial options, help set priorities, and lead clients through the hard choices ahead.[8]

In addition to her organization memberships, Stacy plans unusual networking activities on purpose. She wants the events to encapsulate her brand: intimate, educational, fun, different, and memorable. For example, she hosts various private networking groups:

- Money Circles—A series of five evening sessions attended by 10 to 15 women, all going through divorce, who discuss the issues confronting them and possible solutions. She offers these circles several times a year.
- In May/June and September/October, three to four times a week, she invites seven to ten clients, prospects, colleagues, and referral sources to join her for a NY Harbor sail on her sailboat. Sometimes she hosts referral partners and their invited guests. For every invitee it is a very personal, intimate, memorable experience.

Stacy supplements her in-person group meetings with one-on-one meetings and a robust social media program. She typically has four one-on-ones a week—a large time investment—but her networking pays off: She estimates that 80 percent of her clients come from referrals.

Her networking trajectory from broad-based to niche follows her growth strategy. She went from networking with all kinds of professionals and service providers to a focus on those serving the divorced women market; and from groups created by others to groups that reflect her clientele, her personality, her firm's culture, and her brand.

Rosmarin and Francis are involved in a wide variety of networking endeavors. Networking, in all guises, probably forms a part of every day for them. But does all networking have to be this involved to be effective? Certainly, it's true

8. https://www.divorceandfinance.org/page/Join; https://www.divorceandfinance.org/page/DivorceFP.

that what you get from networking is commensurate with what you put in, but does every successful networker have to do this much?

The answer is *no*. Not all successful networkers have to be active at this very high level. A person can focus his/her networking on one group or one type of referral source. An introvert may avoid big parties and develop meaningful relationships with a handful of people. An extrovert may enjoy a "Pied Piper role"—leading multitudes of people toward shared goals. Ambiverts—those somewhere on the continuum between introvert and extrovert—will create their own combinations of activities.

Many professionals equate networking with specific activities and then define it as comfortable or uncomfortable. You should never purposely put yourself in a situation that makes you feel awkward. Your body language will say you are ill at ease and people will read your actions as insincere or inauthentic. Strategic networking processes are designed to make networking activities less stressful because you are prepared. There are many ways to find comfortable networking situations where networking is a by-product of an activity you enjoy. Think parties, lectures, golf, conferences, little league, hiking.

> "Strategic networking is an 'investment time' strategy. It is a goal-driven process for creating personal relationships that help individuals achieve economic, social, and emotional goals."

Networking is more about focus and attitude than activity and aptitude. Those who benefit from networking activities see a relationship-building process. Strategic networking activates a plan to link their networking activities with strategies designed to move them toward specific goals.

Networking Defined

Strategic networking, as an "investment time" strategy, is a goal-driven process for creating personal relationships that helps individuals achieve economic, social, and emotional goals. It should be an intentional strategy for finding, meeting, and establishing solid relationships with individuals who can introduce you to new ideas, colleagues who can introduce you to people who want to use your services, and potential clients who want to hire you.

On a more emotional level, networking fulfills human beings' need to interact socially in groups. "Networking begins as basic communication between people who share an interest in each other and their business, for the purpose of advancing opportunities for each of those who participate in the network."[9]

Three lawyers I interviewed gave similar definitions:

Roger E. Barton, managing partner of a mid-sized law firm, says networking is all about relationships: "making relationships . . . leveraging relationships . . . learning from others through relationships . . . and always thinking about interconnections—how to put A and B together for their mutual benefit."

David J. Abeshouse, lawyer, arbitrator, and mediator, built his own group to meet a variety of needs. He says, "Customizing your own networking group to me seems better than trying to fit your own round peg into some other folk's square hole." His group is always built around relationships of "like-minded people, who are or become friends, sitting around a table, sharing ideas."

Employment lawyer Richard Friedman's business comes from referrals, so he networks to find and nurture referral relationships. He defines networking as "meeting other people who are interested in expanding their contacts and clientele and with whom I can follow up for our mutual benefit."

Why Network?

People's reasons for networking range from personal quests to new business acquisition. This book emphasizes ways to use networking opportunities to build a business, a career, or a new life. Some people feel that when a personal business goal is part of the reason for networking, it adds a selfishness that taints what should be the altruistic underpinning of networking relationships. In reality, whatever the reasons behind your networking strategies, "paying it forward" is always an important part of any networking plan. Remember, successful networkers help themselves by helping others.

Through networking people develop:

- Allies
- Colleagues
- Friends

9. Lindy Asimus, "Create Your Personal Network Online," August 25, 2017, http://www.designbusinessengineering.com/create_your_personal_network.htm.

- Mentors
- Personal resources
- Professional resources
- Referral sources

In terms of developing business, individuals may want to

- acquire knowledge or competitive intelligence;
- build a business, technical, or personal resource network;
- find new clients;
- raise their visibility among their prospect groups or with their clients or referral sources;
- showcase their expertise; or
- enhance their reputation.

Dan Lear, a lawyer and Director of Industry Relations at Avvo, networks because "he likes people and likes learning from them." He finds or forms groups "built around common interests, passions, and worldview." He looks for "strong connectors to share his energy and enthusiasm in learning about who people are."

Larry Hutcher, co-managing partner at a midsize law firm, learned the basic tenets of networking in college while working summers as a Fuller Brush salesman going door to door and asking "How can I help you?" He says this is basically what he continues to do today.

Jessica Thaler-Parker, an attorney working in regulatory change and project management in NYC, says "Everything is networking. It is about meeting people with different skill sets and experience and not knowing where the connection will lead. I love people and learning about them. I like a big network so I can tap in for work or personal issues and always have someone to reach out to."

Marcia R. Golden analogizes meeting people while networking to dating, and to creating a solid, strong relationship to marriage. At the marriage stage, networkers still "don't sell to one another. Rather, we choose to do business with each other."

Where Does "Strategic" Fit In?

Adding the adjective "strategic" to networking refers to intention—the networkers' intentions to create a planned, cumulative networking plan focused on opportunities that move their goals forward. Three networkers explained their basic strategies:

- Hollace Topol Cohen, a bankruptcy attorney, says "Networking is about establishing the right relationships with people. Business comes from these relationships because people see your integrity through your networking interactions with them."
- For Larry Hutcher, co-managing partner of Davidoff Hutcher & Citron, "Networking for me always occurs in defined group settings where everyone comes with the same purpose. Good networkers are good listeners and good givers. You give first because it always comes back to you."
- David Rosenbaum, head of IT Consulting at Citrin Cooperman, said, "The strategy of networking reflects what is going on in your profession. You need to highlight your unique features and make sure that people who need you can find you."

Strategic networking is a process that happens through a series of integrated steps.

1. You begin with your goals: what you want to do and why you want to do it.
2. You create a plan to fulfill your goals.
3. You identify places where the kinds of people you want to know gather.
4. You then plan a series of networking initiatives that situate you in the places where your target market goes.
5. Relationships grow as, over time, people find points of connection that build a foundation of trust. It is a gradual process that moves strangers forward from their initial handshake to a close connection between friends.

Several interviewees discussed the links between our definition of networking, strategic considerations, and success.

As David J. Abeshouse explains the purpose: "Networking is a way of extending your reach so that your products or services can be known by as many people in your market as possible. It can help you develop new business, but it can also help you meet people who can become important to your business and personal growth in many ways."

Andrew C. Peskoe, a corporate lawyer, explains the benefits of networking very clearly. "You network to keep informed at a level you can't get from media about what is important in the industries you serve. You get introductions to resources you can make available to clients, possible clients, and people who need your services and who may offer business opportunities. Networking is what grows a practice. Provide advice and resources as you get to know people and it leads to work. Don't expect others to imagine you can add value. Just add it."

Lenny Carraturo, commercial business development officer at Wells Fargo Bank, is a connector, a center of influence for accountants, attorneys, wealth advisors, and business owners who need access to his bank's financial resources. His goal is to be viewed as a professional who "wants to help companies become more efficient and increase revenues and profit margins." He always asks, "What are you doing? How can we work together?"

Even with an intentional strategy there is always room for serendipity. You never know when someone you know will introduce you to someone they know who will become your client and friend. Linda Klein, a lawyer and past president of the ABA, tells about the time she did an easy favor for an accountant. Twenty years later, now a business advisor for SCORE, he sent Linda a SCORE client who needed his new business incorporated. That start-up business grew into a successful private company, and continues to be her client.

Networking Strategy

Networking strategy is not etched in stone, nor is it one size fits all. The specifics of a networking strategy morph as your situation and goals change. Your strategy will be grounded in your assessment of what you do, why you do it, and where work fits into your vision of the good life. Your activities will link your goals to specific people, groups, and opportunities. While this focus on yourself and your needs may sound selfish and self-centered, more sales-oriented than collaborative, it is tempered by networking norms that stress cooperation, quality relationships, and mutual benefit.

Beginners often welcome the strict protocols of networking groups like BNI[10] "that can teach them networking etiquette," or general-purpose networking groups that include a broad cross section of businesses and interests. As careers mature, people tend to focus more directly on niche activities or niche markets. Their networking choices shift to mirror their more focused goals. Or people create private groups where networking, learning, and leads are shared with close allies and clients.

Roger E. Barton doesn't participate in general networking groups anymore. He did initially when he looked to acquire clients through referrals; but now, he is focused on building his business by getting to know "end users"—

10. See discussion about BNI in Chapter 5.

potential clients. As with many expert networkers, his networking venues mirror his changing business focus.

Lenny Carraturo is a commercial business development officer at Wells Fargo Bank. Where once he joined general membership groups, he now wants to meet only accountants, attorneys, wealth advisors, and business owners who can introduce him to their clients who need access to his company's financial resources.

Sometimes a networker's strategic direction is influenced by outside forces that cause him/her to seek relationships with new groups. It could be

- a new law or regulation that will create changes for clients who benefit from your practice area, such as changes in immigration policies or changes in wage and hour, tax, or energy laws; or
- a trend that will impact your clients' lives, such as the effect of mobile devices on access to services, or the impact of ride-hailing services on the livelihood of traditional yellow cab drivers.

Often a person's networking strategy reflects career changes. Sometimes people move firms; other times they need to reinvent themselves if their practice areas dry up or they decide some other area is more interesting. Frequently, litigators, tired of litigation stress, shift their practice over to the more controllable areas of mediation and arbitration.

Changes may take place internally within your firm or company that cause you to modify your goals. For example,

- An increasing emphasis on a new practice area such as corporate security, social media, or privacy regulations;
- A decline in your practice area due to external economic conditions; or
- Your own interest in changing the focus of your practice.

Whatever the initiating opportunity, your networking strategy will need to mirror the change. You may need to spend time with different resources and people in your own network or meet new people through your colleagues' networks. Here are examples of a variety of activities that can be combined to implement new strategies:

- Events—attend conferences, meetings, meals.
- Participation—group leadership roles; speeches; working a room; providing thought leadership through blogs, articles, newsletters.
- Paying it forward—use your resource network and personal skill set to help others who will in turn help you.
- Connect with thought leaders in your network or your contacts' networks in order to learn about new areas and opportunities.

Pay It Forward

Regardless of the specific plans you use to convert contacts into friends, allies, colleagues, clients, mentors, or referral sources, successful networking pays it forward. It's less about getting something specific for yourself first and more about thinking of those with whom you network in terms of what *they* want and need, and how you can help *them* achieve their goals. Those who build a reputation as givers, in turn, get.

Larry Hutcher, co-managing partner of a midsize law firm, says, "I ask everyone I meet how I can help them. Then I listen closely, and often I can make a terrible situation less terrible. Good networkers are givers; give first and it will come back to you."

Marc W. Halpert, LinkedIn trainer and business entrepreneur, says the secret to networking success is "assessing what you can do for others before you let them know what they can do for you." He gets a psychic reward whenever he is "able to introduce two people who then do business together and together present a business opportunity to me."

Bernadette Beekman, attorney and Managing Director of Hire Counsel, doesn't like the term "networking." She prefers to call what she does "engagement and personal connections." She "likes people and finding out how I can help them." She defines the best networkers as people who are "fun, happy, pleasant, honest, authentic, and generous."

Interpersonal Relationships

Networking conversations offer a window into how people think and act. Good networkers understand what makes other people tick—what they need in order to create mutually beneficial affiliations. This is why attitude is more important than aptitude.

- Are you interested in the lives of other people?
- Are you interested in how other people build careers, families, and businesses?

If you are, you can be a good networker. Networking works best when you adopt an open mind marked by an interest in others and a willingness to share. Ivan Misner, the founder of BNI Network, notes that "this interest leads to comfort, and that comfort leads to opportunities to provide referrals as they arise, and those referrals lead to business."[11]

11. Ibid.

While you are getting to know people, they are getting to know you. This is especially true in the services world. Professional services become observable during interactions between the professional and the client. Even though service providers have tangible products, they are usually judged on the quality of the intangible shared experience—the chemistry between the provider and the client, the appropriateness of client service, and the value of the shared experience.

> Misner says, '[Networking] isn't something you do to someone—it's something you do with them. It's a conversation.'[12]

Many people believe that behavior in networking situations provides clues as to how those you interact with would be in a work situation.

- If you listen attentively at a party it is assumed you are similarly attuned to your clients' articulation of their needs.
- If you promise to send an article or schedule a breakfast and you do so in a timely manner, it is assumed that you are prompt in your business dealings.
- If you ask intelligent questions during a networking conversation, people assume you are a smart, experienced professional.

The skills and personal attributes that make a good networker are similar to the skills required to be a good professional, a good parent, a good colleague, a good friend. In all environments, success requires

- a psychological approach to dialogue—paying attention to what is said, how it is said and what is unsaid,
- research skills,
- the ability to construct pragmatic strategies around realistic goals,
- empathy—interest in and validation of others' concerns,
- active listening skills,
- asking relevant questions,
- courtesy and good manners, and
- patience and a generosity of spirit—a willingness to listen for and hear the need buried in a conversation and tend to it.

12. Ivan Misner, "Why So Many People Resist Networking and Miss Out," April 11, 2013, https://www.entrepreneur.com/article/226359.

Networking Time Is an Investment

Business development—networking, marketing, public relations—should be viewed as building blocks in your networking strategy. Your networking is an investment that provides a path to implement your goals. You build up from your goals by joining appropriate groups and planning one-on-one meetings with individuals you can help who can also help you.

As with financial investments, attaining a goal takes time. It may take several years to move from strangers shaking hands to colleague and trusted advisor. It may take 20 years, as a client of mine once explained. He met a potential client 20 years earlier and then faithfully kept in touch with the man. Fast forward 20 years and a young associate meets the man, identifies a solution to one of his current problems, and brings him into the firm as a client. My client said, "C'est la vie."

Networking is a long-term strategy. It requires time to plan and time for the plans to come to fruition. The shift from stranger to friend, according to a study about friendship,

> usually takes roughly 50 hours of time together to go from acquaintance to "casual friend" (think drinking buddies, or friends of friends that you see at parties); around 90 hours to become a true-to-form "friend" (you both carve out time to specifically hang out with one another); and over 200 hours to form a BFF-type bond (you feel an emotional connection with this friend).[13]

The strategic part of networking preparations takes time. For example, if you approach networking events as a three-part process [see Chapter 10], attendance at a networking meeting or event can take anywhere from three to six hours.

- Pre-activity research and personal preparation: one-half hour to one and one-half hours
- Travel to and from event: one to two hours
- The activity itself: one to two and one-half hours
- Follow-up: half an hour to an hour

Because each networking activity will take time to plan and time to implement, your selection of appropriate opportunities should be laser focused. All your networking choices should cumulatively move you toward your goals. This is the reason to adhere to your strategic networking plans.

Of course, sometimes an opportunity may seem perfect, and turn out to be less than it seemed. To mitigate the number of blind alleys you walk down, and

---

13. Patrick Allan, "It Takes 90 Hours to Make a New Friend," April 10, 2018, https://lifehacker.com/it-takes-90-hours-to-make-a-new-friend-1825145592.

to make efficient use of your time, turn to your goals to create an underlying theme that links each initiative into a series of coordinated interactions.

The specific places you go and the people you target will evolve as you

- research the details about the activities and interests of your targets,
- identify people you wish to meet,
- find them,
- meet them,
- create relationships over time,
- form trust-based rapport with key individuals,
- help them move toward their goals, and
- accomplish your goals.

Sidebar 1.2 What Networking Is Not

- *Meetings are not networking.*
- *Lunch is not networking.*
- *Events are not networking, although networking may occur in any of these venues.*

Networking is not a specific tactic, nor does it need to happen only at a specific time and place.

It is not

- *selling,*
- *participating in random acts of lunch,*
- *speed-meeting,*
- *gathering the maximum number of business cards per meeting, or*
- *promoting your services like a used-car salesman.*

Many people who fear networking characterize it as

- *boring, a waste of time or a time suck,*
- *embarrassing,*
- *salesy,*
- *humdrum chit-chat, or*
- *wasted time away from work.*

Going Forward: Book Contents

The process begins by recognizing opportunities. In this book we discuss how to

- create a plan keyed to your goals;
- create networks of contacts;

- use networking tools, such as target personas, elevator speeches, and value propositions, to communicate your message to your target audience; and
- select from an array of venues—both online and in-person—that put you in touch with members of your target audience or people who can refer you to those targets.

We then look at important aspects of the networking process:

- the tangible and intangible preparations that precede networking initiatives;
- the etiquette of personal networking;
- the art of referrals; and
- best practices for integrating, evaluating, and measuring activities.

Guided by this information and advice from the expert networkers interviewed for this book, you will be able to develop your own set of comfortable networking activities and useful approaches.

Creating a Research-Based Action Plan

2

Networking strategies offer opportunities to create the first personal linkages among providers, referrers, and potential clients. The question is not should I network? Rather it is, how given all the available networking possibilities, can I create relationships with the people who are right for me at this time in my life and my career?

The answer is to create a networking strategy.

The difference between ad hoc networking activities that may or may not pan out and strategically cumulative networking initiatives is a plan. A plan is an important document for many reasons:

- It includes goals that point separate undertakings toward a common end.
- It prioritizes strategies, assigning time and money resources to each one.
- It includes metrics to evaluate the value of specific initiatives.
- It keeps you grounded and focused on where you need to go and why.

Most of the networkers interviewed for this book have a specific goal-based strategy that informs their networking decisions. Examples include the following:

Stacey Cohen, CEO of a marketing communications firm, works with clients in five industries, so she wants to interact with higher-level executives, CEOs, and business owners in those industries.

Roger E. Barton, managing partner of Barton LLP, concentrates his networking in three organizations where he meets potential clients: (1) Primerus, an international association of law firms, (2) the British-American Business Association, and (3) an educational institute he founded that provides programs for in-house counsel.

Martin S. Klein, a trust and estates attorney, is active in two kinds of groups: attorney-dominated groups where he meets lawyers who become referral partners, and general membership groups where he meets other professionals who can be both referrers and resources for his clients.

In this chapter we discuss the process for developing goals and creating an action plan that moves you toward your goals. The plan should have three key components:

- Clearly defined goals
- A SWOT [strengths, weaknesses, opportunities, threats] analysis to identify strategic opportunities and obstacles
- An action plan that
    - establishes guidelines for when, where, and how to expend your time and money;
    - integrates and prioritizes your goals, strategies, and tactics; and
    - creates metrics to gauge the value of specific activities

Steps in the Planning Process

Figure 2.1 shows the steps in the planning process. The four-step process includes two research steps followed by two action steps. The two research steps are:

1. Research about yourself, your career/life plans, helpful and inhibiting factors related to your workplace, and your social interaction preferences.
2. A SWOT analysis, which is a four-quadrant summary of your own *strengths* and *weaknesses* juxtaposed to the situation in the world outside that presents both *opportunities* and *threats*.

The two action steps are:

1. Setting pragmatic, realistic, doable goals that can be tracked and measured.
2. Preparing a marketing action plan that assigns strategies and tactics to each goal.

Figure 2.1 Steps in the Planning Process

Your Context	SWOT Analysis	Goal-Setting	Marketing Action Plan
personal preferences work/career plans assets/ liabilities of firm/company social interaction preferences	YOU: strengths weaknesses OUTSIDE WORLD: opportunities threats	SMART goals specific measurable attainable relevant time-based maximum of 3 goals	two strategies per goal two tactics for each strategy

The worksheets found in Appendix 2, pages 185–192, will guide you through the specific content for each step.

Setting the Context

Selecting appropriate goals begins with constructing a **context** in which to place the goals. This process begins with a self-assessment of your preferred work-life and personal-life choices. These choices create the base upon which you will build your plan.

Research Begins with YOU

GPS keeps us on the right road, but only when we input the correct destination. So, too, with business development and career growth. First, you need to identify a destination. If you don't know where you are starting from or what your goals are, you are liable to find yourself facing dead ends.

Networking strategies should be closely tied to your career and life goals, where you think you are on the introvert–extrovert continuum, your personal preferences regarding meeting and talking to people, and your ambition and curiosity. The series of worksheets found in Appendix 2, pages 185–192, are designed to help you assess these issues.

Begin by answering the personal questions in Worksheet 2.1 Personal Preferences: Work-Life Balance [Appendix 2, pages 185–186]. The questions relate to the relative importance of work and non-work as parts of your life.

You also need to look at specific aspects of your work environment:

- First, aspects of your present situation
- Then, your future "druthers"

You want to think about what you like to do and what kind of people you like to work for and with. Ask yourself where, when, and how you want your life and your career to intersect. To get started, answer the questions in Worksheet 2.2 Your Work [Appendix 2, page 187] as honestly, realistically, and thoughtfully as you can. The questions refer to specifics about your work including the type of work you do, the kind of clients you work with, what you like and don't like about work, and what changes you would make if you could.

Now that you have thought about your own work and the clients you work with, the next worksheet, Worksheet 2.3 Assets and Liabilities of the Company/Firm You Work For [Appendix 2, page 188], asks you to review the larger picture of the assets and liabilities of the entity you work for in order to see which aspects may help or hinder attainment of your goals.

The firm or company creates a major part of the context in which you develop your networking strategies. You want to pay attention to the entity's brand, resources, client base, and competitors.

- The **brand** represents the history, activities, and reputation of the entity you work for. Think Enron versus Goldman Sachs. The higher the brand value, the easier it is for you to use it as a base for your own networking activities.
- **Resources** refer to the physical and cultural support for personal marketing activities. Does your firm value and promote personal marketing initiatives? Does the firm pay for group memberships, conference expenses, firm-sponsored networking activities?
- **Client base** refers to the kind of clients you work with and would like to work with in the future. The characteristics of your best clients will become characteristics of your networking target.
- **Competitors** are those individuals, companies, and firms that rival or outshine the entity you work for.

Brand, resources, client base, and competitors will all impact your own business development efforts. For example:

- If your firm has strong brand awareness and large market share, this can be an advantage for you.

- If your firm's client base includes many companies or individuals who could use your services if they knew they were available, this can be an advantage for you.
- If another professional in your firm has a strong brand and presence in your practice area, you will need to find a way to differentiate yourself.
- If your firm is struggling for market share, this could make it more difficult to grow your own practice.

Worksheet 2.4 Social Interaction Preferences [Appendix 2, page 189] focuses again on you. This time in terms of your social preferences. Networking is about developing and maintaining close personal relationships, so you need to think about your attitude toward and aptitude for social interaction. Networking activities run the gamut from one-on-one meetings to large events. What kind of group situation do you prefer?

Some people don't want to "give to get." Others feel like they have no resources or contacts that would be of interest to other people. You need to assess honestly your willingness to put yourself out to meet other people and help them attain their goals. Use Worksheet 2.4 to consider these sometimes-difficult questions.

Where are you on the introvert–extrovert scale? While anyone can learn to network, introverts tend to use different approaches than extroverts to increase their effectiveness. For example, extroverts may move through parties high fiving and asking basic how are you questions, while introverts may prefer to settle down with one person for an in-depth conversation.

SWOT: Strengths, Weaknesses, Opportunities, and Threats Matrix

Once you have completed Worksheets 2.1 through 2.4 you will have enough basic information to create a one-page summary of the pluses and minuses that will affect attainment of your goals. Use Worksheet 2.5 SWOT Analysis [Appendix 2, page 190] to present all the factors you think may impact movement toward your goals.

Following is a sample of the kinds of questions you need to include in the SWOT. Look back to your answers in the worksheets and then include those ideas in this analysis. When you are finished you should have a comparison of your situation vis-à-vis the context in which you will approach networking. This analysis will help you determine your networking target, your message for your target, and your available resources.

Worksheet 2.5 SWOT Analysis with Sample Questions

Strengths*	**Opportunities****
What are you good at? Why do people hire you? How do clients benefit from the work you do for them? How are you different from others who practice in the same area?	What trends, legislation, laws, or court decisions are on the horizon that can make your goals more relevant to potential clients? Where are the best places to grow your practice? Where are the kinds of clients you want to work with?
Weaknesses	**Threats**
What attitudes and habits interfere with your work life? What resources will you need that you don't have now? What new subjects will you need to master? What new skills will you need to acquire?	What threats are there in your work environment? What threats may emerge in your private life? What trends could adversely impact your plans? Who are the competitors already in the space you want to occupy?

*NOTE: Strengths and weaknesses refer to you in the context of the questions answered in Worksheets 2.1 through 2.4.
**NOTE: Opportunities and threats deal with phenomena in the external environment.

Goal Setting

Once you have completed Worksheets 2.1–2.5, you are ready to draw a big picture, personal preferences canvas on which to paint specific goals and the strategies necessary to achieve them. Saying you want more business is an aspirational goal. A viable goal is realistic, detailed, and definable, such as:

- I want to acquire two corporate clients in the energy industry in need of counsel concerning interstate contracts.
- I want to double the amount of work I do for my two largest clients.
- I want five new clients in the renewable energy sector.

One way to come to grips with specificity is to remember the SMART[1] goal-setting acronym:

S = specific [be precise in your language]
M = measure [be able to quantify or estimate qualitatively]
A = attainable [possible to achieve]
R = relevant [consistent with your goals]
T = time-based [due dates, time line]

Keeping this mnemonic in mind can help you to distinguish "druthers" from actionable initiatives.

Use Worksheet 2.6 Goal Setting [Appendix 2, page 191] to set out one to three specific, measurable, achievable goals to move toward in the next 12 months. A year may sound like a long time, but in practice, it can take that long to develop the close relationships that lead to new business.

To make the path to your goals more realistic, subdivide your major goal into segments that have three- to six-month time frames. Choose only one goal to begin if that makes you more comfortable. If you have more than three goals it is hard to find time to move them all forward.

A few hints:

- If you decide to have monetary goals in addition to a dollar amount, you might want to specify percentages to come from new clients and/or from additional work from current or past clients.
- If you want to add new clients, be specific in terms of the clients' key characteristics and the nature of the work they want you to do for them.
- If you want current clients to add additional kinds of work, specify the new areas of work and why they would want you to do it for them. You may want to indicate the client(s) and the services.
- If you have work–life balance goals, you may want to identify the time management initiatives that will be required to achieve this balanced life.
- If you have personal goals, such as intellectual or subject matter challenges, you may want to tie those goals to others related to expanding or changing your work focus.

1. It is generally accepted that the SMART acronym was first written down in November 1981, in Spokane, Washington when George T. Doran, a consultant and former director of corporate planning for Washington Water Power Company published a paper titled "There's a S.M.A.R.T. Way to Write Management's Goals and Objectives." Duncan Haughey, "A Brief History of Smart Goals," December 13, 2014, https://www.projectsmart.co.uk/brief-history-of-smart-goals.php.

Putting a Plan Together

Now you have formulated a realistic assessment of your world and your first set of goals. The final step is to write an action plan that adds the strategies and tactics you will use to achieve the goals. The purpose of a plan is

- to think entrepreneurially about growing your practice,
- to provide the nuts and bolts of a strategic marketing plan, and
- to increase your business opportunities by building the process around your goals.

It's a truism that people hire people they know, like, and trust. Usually those people are similar in important ways to each other. Through strategic networking you can identify those people, locate them, and learn how they prefer to gather information and make choices. Of course, the final step is then to go where they go and meet with them.

In your plan, you will want to lay out your intentions for identifying and connecting with people from different parts of your life. Think about the following people:

- Current clients with the potential to use more services
- Current clients who can introduce you to potential clients
- Referral sources both in and outside your place of business
- End-users who could become clients

Your intentions could include the following strategies:

- Become visible to potential clients
- Become known as an experienced, savvy, successful practitioner in your chosen area
- Increase the quality of your referrer base
- Create a social media presence that reinforces your in-person networking activities
- Become comfortable and accepted in your target market
- Broaden and/or deepen the connections in your network

Use Worksheet 2.7 Marketing Action Plan [Appendix 2, page 192] to create your written plan. Writing it down helps you think in terms of the whole process—where you want to begin and where you want to end. A consultant colleague of mine says that "written plans are also easier to share with others, easier to review and modify as time goes on, easier as gauges of your progress and execution, and easier to hold yourself accountable."

To begin, carry the goals over from Worksheet 2.6. For each goal you will develop one or two strategies designed to reach the goal.

In the action plan, you will map out a series of strategies and tactics to move toward your goals. Strategies and tactics are complementary, like Dick and Jane, Mutt and Jeff, Abbott and Costello. They work together but serve different functions.

Strategies are broader than tactics.

- Strategies identify in broad strokes where you need to go to achieve a goal. They point the way.
- Strategies focus activities and initiatives so that you can accomplish more in less time.
- Strategies turn goals into realities.

Tactics are the details, the to-dos that implement strategies. Strategies help you identify target audiences; tactics finds the specific place where those people congregate. For each strategy, you should identify one or two tactics.

- Tactics are specific to-dos that when executed accomplish the strategy or move it forward [See "List of Possible Tactics" Appendix 3, page 209].
- Selecting a specific networking group or trade association conference is a tactic.
- Tactics include plans to attend specific group meetings, make dates with specific individuals, set time lines and due dates, write articles, speak at conferences, and so on.

Select your tactics carefully so that they maximize your ability to interact with people who can help you to grow. You want to limit your goals, strategies, and tactics to fit your resources—time, money, outside assistance. It is better to work on one goal effectively than three goals nominally.

You will also want to coordinate your activities so that the impact on your target audience is cumulative. For example, if you want your target audience to know more about your expertise as a litigator with extensive experience in product liability cases, you could do any or all of the following:

- Identify and join specific groups and organizations where your target audience goes for believable advice and information.
    - Plan how you will become a part of the group's community. For example, you could join a local chapter committee, volunteer to write an article for their newsletter or blog, or volunteer to host a panel or be a speaker at their annual conference.
- Identify four to six people in the groups you join whom you want to get to know.
    - Make dates with them to have a beer after a meeting or meet on a separate day for coffee.

    - Begin to think about people you might introduce them to or information you might send them.
- Identify four to six appropriate referral sources:
    - Other professionals who work with your target audience
    - Contacts who work at your best clients who could introduce you to their contacts at similar firms
    - Colleagues and vendors who also work with your best clients
- Check if LinkedIn has an online group that is the same as the in-person group you plan to join, and if so, join it. Then set aside time each week to check the discussions and contribute to one discussion in a way that showcases your expertise.
- Search for online sites and groups where your target audience goes and join them. Participate in a similar fashion.

Some tips:

- People buy expertise, so when you think of marketing, think of it in terms of specific proficiencies that your niche groups may be interested in using.
- Spend 80 percent of your time building relationships and 20 percent building your reputation.
- Planning ahead and writing the plan are important preconditions for actually following through with the plan specifics.
- Review your plan quarterly and make adjustments to take advantage of opportunities as they occur or to amend or drop unsuccessful initiatives.

Interviewees' Strategies

Many of the successful networkers I interviewed began their business development networking forays looking for anyone, anywhere. As they built their networks they realized how much time they wasted going to the wrong venues looking for the wrong people. They became more discriminating, cutting down on quantity and looking for higher value connections.

- When David J. Abeshouse, an attorney, first went into solo practice as a litigator he would go to 20 or more networking activities a week, looking anywhere and everywhere for referrers or clients. Often, he was "lookin' for love in all the wrong places."[2] As he gradually morphed his practice from litigation to mediation and arbitration, including as a neutral arbitrator and mediator, he cut down his activity level. He now participates in fewer groups and looks for the value and quality in the contacts he spends time with.

- David Rosenbaum, a technology consultant, says his strategy has always reflected what is going on in his profession. In the 1980s, no one really knew what to do with computers, so he had to provide information and plant seeds. By 2000, computers had become ubiquitous and his strategy morphed accordingly from teaching about the product to creating available resources for clients. Today, potential clients are once again confused by all the options and he is again in teaching mode, planting seeds.
- James K. Landau, a litigator, concentrates on meeting individuals who are lawyers or who can refer him to lawyers. When he meets them, he articulates the benefits of referring business to him when they are conflicted out of the work or are uncomfortable taking a particular case. For example, in the beginning, he decided to focus his activities around his local bar association. One day, his committee co-chair introduced him to her husband who was conflicted out of a case. The referral became one of his biggest cases.
- Marcia Sloman, a professional organizer who helps people detach from their possessions, initially looked for business "anywhere and everywhere." Today she focuses on therapist referrers because she found that often one manifestation of their clients' problems is clutter.

In each of these examples, the networkers' strategies maximized connections relevant to their goals by concentrating their efforts on the most meaningful associations. Strategic changes reflected their understanding of their practice strengths and their assessment as to the best available opportunities.

Chapter Summary

Creating a marketing action plan allows you to gain control over the growth of your practice and your career and focus on what interests you. You can concentrate your efforts on clearly identified audiences and niches.

Interacting with defined target groups lets you learn their habits, preferences, and jargon. You will be able to learn the nuances and details of their environments. At the same time, they will learn about you and the relevance of your

2. "Lookin' for Love" is a song written by Wanda Mallette, Bob Morrison, and Patti Ryan, and recorded by American country music singer Johnny Lee. It was released in June 1980 as part of the soundtrack to the film *Urban Cowboy*. https://en.wikipedia.org/wiki/Lookin%27_for_Love.

expertise to their needs. The result will be opportunities to cultivate meaningful relationships with people you can help to succeed and who, in turn, will want to help you succeed.

We will now turn to some "how" chapters: how to create a contacts base, how to assess in-person and online groups in order to find the most appropriate ones for you, and how to prepare yourself and your materials to make a memorable impression.

Who's in Your Network? 3

Everybody has a network. We are born into one—our family. As we grow, our network expands and evolves, reflecting our aspirations and life choices. Some links in our network just happen, other parts we develop consciously. When you think about it, your network includes relationships from three time periods:

- Your past—all the people you used to know or who knew you
- Your present—all the people you know today, including some you may not want to know, and some you don't know who know you
- Your future—all the people you would like to know

When we decide to consciously construct a network, this purposeful network is usually intended to further a specific idea or goal. Susan Duncan summed up the importance of purposeful networks saying, "The quality of a network and how it is used is critical. . . . Effective networking generates referrals to more 'ideal' clients, provides competitive intelligence, opens up leadership opportunities, helps with personal and professional growth and helps you grow your practice."[1]

In this chapter we look at various kinds of networks and how to build them.

Network Components

When we want to build or rebuild a network we draw from three primary streams of people,[2] as shown in Figure 3.1, often beginning with personal connections, adding occupational and aspirational.

1. Susan Duncan, "Women's Success Strategies for Advancement," https://www.linkedin.com/pulse/womens-success-strategies-advancement-susan-saltonstall-duncan/.

2. Adapted from Linda Hill and Kent Lineback, "The Three Networks You Need," blogs, *Harvard Business Review*, March 3, 2011, https://hbr.org/2011/03/the-three-networks-you-need.html.

Figure 3.1 Network Components

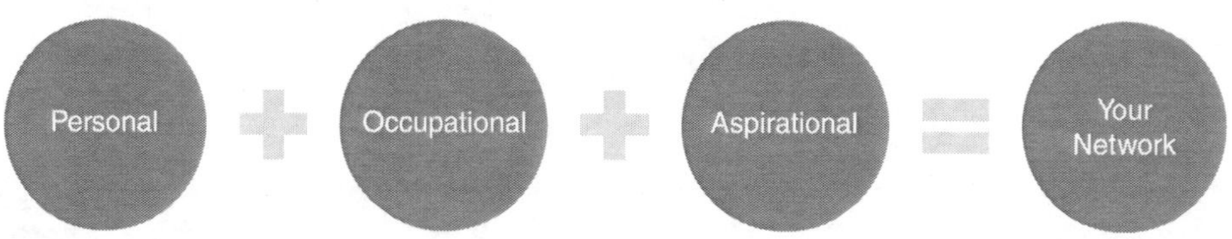

Personal Networks

Typically, people begin to build a network around their comfort base—family, close friends, and mentors. These bonds are the deepest and most personal—the people you go to for advice and sympathy, the ones you touch base with at major choice points in your personal life or career.

Usually, the friends and family network expands without strategic thought. Individuals in this network include the following:

- Family—parents, siblings, relatives, spouses, and their networks of relatives
- Friends—people you meet and bond with in school, at work, playing sports, sharing hobbies, and their families
- Mentors—family members you look to for guidance, teachers, clergy, people in charge in your workplace, coaches, tutors
- Neighbors
- Military service friendships
- People who work in stores you frequent
- Your lawyer, accountant, financial planner, doctors
- Members of social, civic, religious, and community groups to which you belong

This personal group grows over time to include people you employ for personal care or household needs, for example, a personal trainer, hair stylist, cook, house cleaner, dog walker, tailor, plumber, electrician, contractor. As your family grows, so, too, your vendor network multiplies to include babysitters, child care professionals, tutors, coaches. You also have your personal doctors, bankers, brokers, and lawyers.

Occupational Networks

These include colleagues in your firm, as well as clients who depend on you for their success, and outside vendors who work with your clients or provide services for you and your firm. Begin by thinking about people within your personal workplace circle.

- Coworkers in your current or former workplaces: those you report to, those who report to you, and those who support your business such as administrative personnel, controller, technology specialist, marketing professional, and so on
- Colleagues in your current or former office, business or firm
- Your former bosses
- Your friends' and family's current and former workplace colleagues, bosses, and vendors
- Clients you work with now or have worked with in the past

Moving out from close connections that touch your work life directly there are also a wide variety of professionals and service vendors you come into contact with through your work. These include the following:

- Professionals in your workplace in other practice areas
- Professionals in complementary professions such as accounting, financial planning, law, information technology, insurance, consulting
- Vendors who sell to people you work with or know
- Experts you meet through client work or at continuing education classes
- People you meet while networking through organizations such as trade associations, professional associations, civic groups, and charities

Aspirational Networks

This is your brain-builder network. It includes people with expertise in your own field, areas you want to learn more about, or fields you might consider entering. People in your aspirational network can help you develop the skills and obtain the knowledge needed to succeed.

These individuals are often futurists, people who study trends and predict changes that may impact your current career and, potentially, future careers. They may be successful business executives or innovators. Some will come from your personal networks, teaching you new hobbies or life skills such as kayaking, gardening, or meditation. Others will be workplace thought leaders, visionaries, trainers, or coaches.

> "You may meet people to include in your aspirational network at conferences or community events or follow footnotes and references that lead you to them. Many will be recommended by people in your other networks."

This network could include people who work in media outlets, think tanks, and government agencies. Many come to your attention through social media, offering ways to follow them online through postings, blogs, newsletters, and white papers. Websites such as LinkedIn offer lists of experts whom you can follow.

Obviously, each network includes past as well as current relationships, for example, post-divorce "exes," people in your old neighborhood or your old job. Considering past encounters, a rule of thumb in terms of thinking about people from your past is to assume that if you remember a person with enough specificity to want to include them in your network, then they, too, probably remember you.

Network Ties: Strong versus Weak

Effective networks need a balance of both strong and weak ties. Strong ties link to our comfort zone; weak ties lead you toward new ideas, new encounters, and new pursuits.

- *Strong ties* bind you with the small number of close relationships that form the core of your support group. Strong ties are people you know well, those you keep in touch with. They tend to share your interests, assumptions, and biases, and so you tend to communicate freely with them. You need best friends, but if your network only includes people like you, you probably will have less access to new ideas and opportunities.
- *Weak ties* connect you with acquaintances or friends of friends. Weak ties are people on your holiday card list, people whose business card you keep just in case, friends of friends in your LinkedIn contacts list. "[S]omeone you know cursorily or historically or maybe even through a network of friends. Someone you used to work with, someone whose kid was on your kid's soccer team 10 years ago, a former neighbor, an acquaintance in a professional group. And strangely, it's someone who can make a difference."[3]

> "People who network strategically make use of both their strong and weak ties; the former for support, the latter to bring in new information."

Typically, people think about their strong ties when they think about networks, without considering the advantages of using your network to learn about new ideas, new trends, new laws. Weak ties bring these kinds of new insights into your network.

When you look at charts showing network relationships you can see the importance of weak ties in creating linkages between pods of personal, strong

3. Marc Miller, "To Get a Job, Use Your Weak Ties," August 17, 2016, https://forbes.com/sites/nextavenue/2016/08/17/to-get-a-job-use-your-weak-ties/#2619254a6b87.

networks. "Weak ties are crucial in binding groups of strong ties together. They bring circles of networks into contact with each other, strengthening relationships and forming new bonds between relationship circles."[4]

Network Support Levels: Instrumental or Psychosocial

Another way of assessing network linkages is in terms of the form of psychological support they provide. Liane Davey, cofounder and principal at 3COze Inc., a team-building and leadership training company, identifies two complementary network types that provide different levels of support.[5]

- *Instrumental support* refers to the "ideas, advice and assistance offered by people trying to help you achieve your goals."[6] People who offer instrumental support are typically found in larger, technology-enabled networks that include many people linked together by weak ties. They offer support without closeness.
- *Psychosocial support* she defines as "the support your network gives you to help you survive and thrive as a person."[7] These are the "deep" connections with people who have known you for a long time—usually family members, close colleagues and friends, or mentors. This is your emotional support network that can help you work through private issues, resolve career worries, or just provider a de-stressor moment during the day.

In her research Davey found that people tend to focus more on just one of these networks instead of seeing them as interrelated assets to be built simultaneously. In my interviews, I noticed that strategic networkers interviewed for this book instinctively tap into both kinds of ties.

- Strong ties as the core of their referral circles and private peer-to-peer networking groups
- Weak ties when they are job hunting, identifying resources for themselves or others, or asking friends to introduce them to specific people in their friends' networks

4. Eileen Brown, "Strong and Weak Ties: Why Your Weak Ties Matter," June 30, 2011, https://socialmediatoday.com/content/strong-and-weak-ties-why-your-weak-ties-matter

5. Liane Davey, "Everyone's Network Should Provide Two Things," *Harvard Business Review*, September 30, 2016, https://hbr.org/2016/09/everyones-network-should-provide-two-things.

6. Ibid.

7. Ibid.

For example, Larry Hutcher, the managing partner and major rainmaker of a mid-size law firm, relies on his "ties with five really important relationships," but at the same time he responds to requests for help from even the weakest ties in his network.

Building Your Own Network

Where you begin depends on where you want to go, which is why you need to do some of the planning in Chapter 2 before you wade into the wide world of network building. Tying your networking opportunities to a specific goal or strategy—be it long or short term—grounds and focuses you so that your networking associations will be cumulatively more effective and helpful.

Think of networking as forming connections with people and organizations to help you move your strategies forward. Remember these are *relationships,* built on reciprocity. As you learn about others, you will look for ways to help them reach their goals and they will do the same for you, so you want to make connections in situations where you will feel comfortable enough to share resources.

Theoretically, the size of any network is infinite. If you assume that you could ask any of your networking contacts to introduce you to any of their close contacts, and if you assume that every person has at least 50 close contacts, the possibilities are overwhelming. We condense this network geometry into the saying that there are "six degrees of separation" between people; meaning that you can meet anyone you want by moving through a chain of "friends of friends."

But time is finite. You don't have time to wade through thousands of possibilities to find the perfect additions to your network. You won't have to if you ground your network building in your goals. So how do you develop a meaningful network of people you value and who will value you? Who are the people you want to build strong relationships with in order to advance your goals?

Jeffrey A. Blutstein, a financial advocate I interviewed, said, "You need to distinguish between the art and science of networking. Who to focus on is art."

In my interviews with three dozen high-performing networkers, I found that key relationships morph depending on where you are in your career and how you want your network to help you.

When Stacy Francis opened Francis Financial 15 years ago, she cast a wide net to grow her business. After becoming a Certified Divorce Financial Analyst™ (CDFA™) she decided to narrow her networking from women in general to a niche market centered on divorced or widowed women in order to help them "find and maintain stable financial footing while undergoing various transitions in their lives." Her networking direction reflects this decision. For example, she ended her leadership of the broad-based, multi-occupation group Allied Professional Women and focused her efforts on the New York City chapter of Association of Divorce Financial Planners' (ADFP) Greater New York Metro Chapter, of which she is the Chapter Director. The switch enabled her to focus her leadership talents on a primary referrer pool.

David J. Abeshouse, a lawyer mediator, and arbitrator, narrowed his networking activities when he changed his legal practice focus to mediation and arbitration, and became more "discriminating . . . looking for value and quality in new contacts." The shift also reflects the difference in marketing practice areas. Mediators and arbitrators have to disclose if they know anyone related to a case before they can be appointed, so dispersed networking is no longer advantageous.

Bonnie Hagen, chief operating officer of Bright Energy Services, "used to cast a really wide net. Now I have a more specific focus because I know who I don't want."

Bernadette Beekman, managing director at Hire Counsel, an attorney temporary placement firm, is totally networked into the female attorney universe. She holds visible leadership positions on the Committee on Women in the Legal Profession at the NYC Bar where she co-chairs the Business and Leadership Subcommittee and is a founding board member of the NYC branch of UPWARD, which encourages connectivity among senior women in all industries worldwide. She is also an active member of the Association of Black Women Attorneys. These networks enable her to continue to contribute to her personal interest in equality for women, and, at the same time, to offer access to many potential clients for her company's temp services.

Building a Goal-Oriented Contacts List

To begin building your network, look through old address books and birthday lists, college and graduate school yearbooks, directories from past and present companies you've worked with, school PTAs, local boards, clubs, and so on. Once these lists have "primed the pump," you can use online databases such as LinkedIn to reconnect and then see who these contacts know that you would like to add as contacts.

There is no magic number of people you should have in your network. Your goal will influence both your networking activities and the people you want to network with. But you should be adding people all the time as you meet them through work or personal events. Add people you meet who are interesting. After a seminar, if you liked the speaker send him or her an invitation to connect on LinkedIn. If you read a stimulating article or blog send the person an invitation to connect online or email them to see if they want to meet in person for coffee. It is always polite when inviting a stranger to connect to reference your link to them—why you would like them to be one of your contacts.

Hollace Topol Cohen, a bankruptcy attorney, said when she was considering a move to her current firm, she became more attracted to the new opportunity as she uncovered positive connections between the new firm and people in her network whose opinion she values, including former colleagues, former clients, and current referral sources.

Let's look at two examples of ways to use you contacts database as part of a specific goal-oriented strategy: career move networking and industry or company searches.

Career Move Networking

Who would you network with if you want to advance your career? Of course, you begin by talking to your close contacts for reassurance and support. But then, think past this part of your network to your weak links—people with new ideas and areas of influence who can introduce you to their network. Some options:

- Look through your college or law school alumni lists to find people who are working in an area or at a firm you think would interest you. To restart a connection reach out to them.
  - You can contact them directly to suggest reconnecting.
  - You can look through their online contacts to find mutual friends. Then ask one of those contacts to re-introduce you.
- Research the career paths of your mentors to find one who has experience in the area you want to learn about. Again, connect and ask for an "information interview" to learn more about his or her experience in the field and what you would need to do to make this kind of move.
- Look through the contacts of your Facebook friends or LinkedIn colleagues to find people whose career or current workplace interests you.

Then ask for introductions so you can question them about how they made career moves and what advice they can give you.
- Similarly, talk to people in your in-person groups for ideas about useful connections and career strategies.

Figure 3.2 highlights five categories of contacts and suggests who you might be looking for, why those specific people, and what you might want to ask them to do to help you.

Figure 3.2 Career Move Networking Opportunities

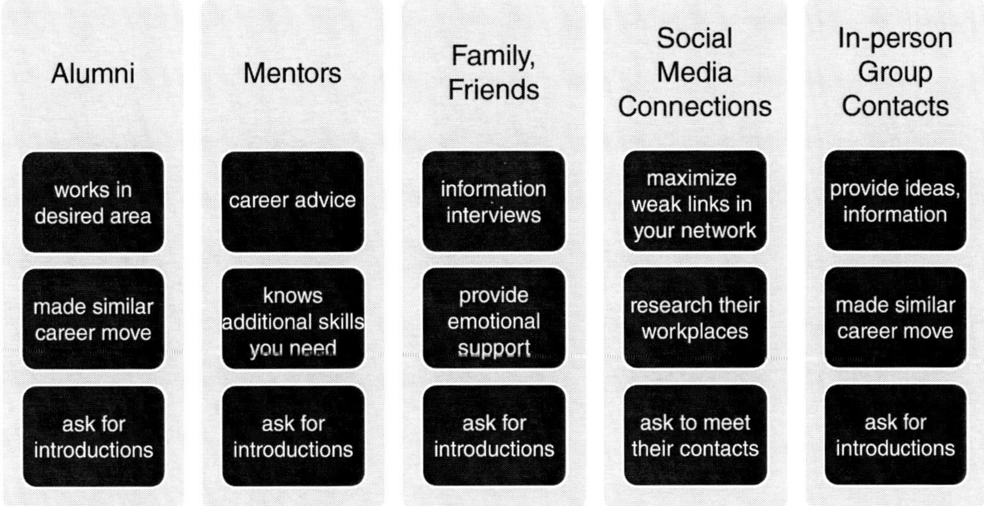

One of the positive outcomes of network-based career research is the opportunity to reconnect with "lost" friends and make new friends. These can lead you to new experiences and ideas.

Industry or Company Searches

Perhaps you want to learn more about a specific industry or company. As Figure 3.3 shows, you can augment online research with in-person discussions, especially with those among your aspirational contacts. People are usually willing to give advice and talk about their own experiences, so make the effort and ask for 15 minutes of their time. To locate these people:

- Use online directories to find people already in your network with experience in the industry or company you are interested in and then connect with them to learn more.

- Join a relevant industry, trade or professional association, as discussed in Chapter 5, to meet people in the industry and learn what is important to them.
- When you find companies you are interested in, ask people already in your network to introduce you to people in their networks who are familiar with that company's culture and organization.

Figure 3.3 Industry or Business-Specific Networking

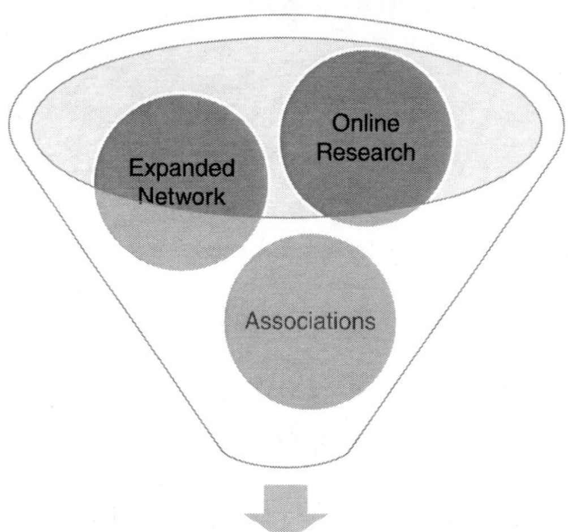

Ask them to make introductions
Offer insights

Your Networking Contacts Database

As shown in Figure 3.4, your contacts database contains four categories of contacts:

- The handful of close contacts in your primarily personal database.
- Ten to twenty contacts you are currently interested in, which we call "top of mind" contacts because you want them to think of you first when they need something you can provide.
- Forty to fifty people you come in contact with on a regular basis in your networking groups, community activities, and so on. Because they see you with some regularity, they are abreast of your current goals.
- Everyone else. The pool from which you draw replacements for your closer relationship categories.

Figure 3.4 Bringing Contacts into Focus

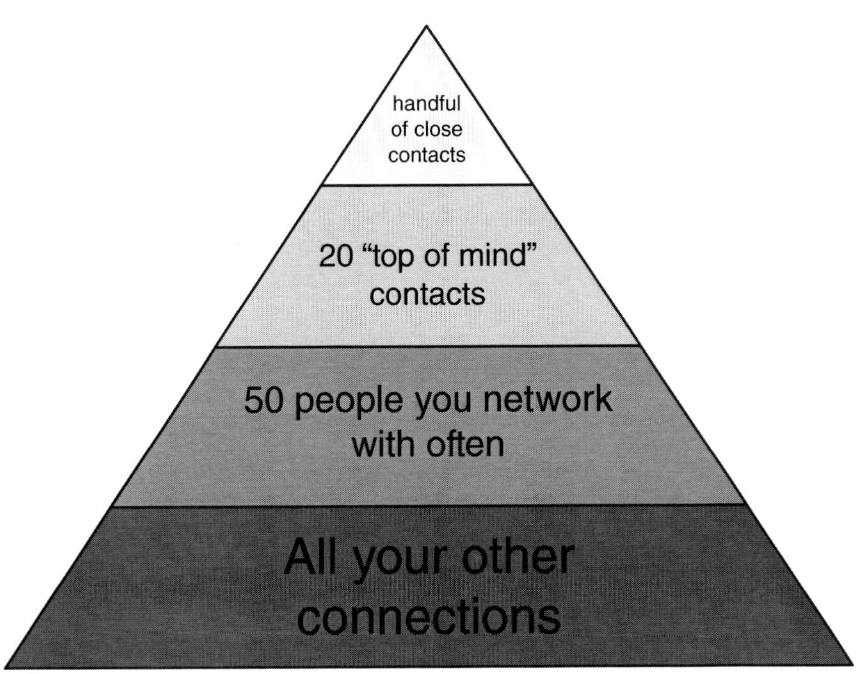

Membership in these four groupings is dynamic. People continually move between categories as their issues, interests, and goals change. A co-worker you lunch with daily may be in your handful of close contacts, until the day she changes jobs. A top of mind client contact may move into the everyone else category when you no longer work with their employer. Those 20 people you saw regularly at monthly in-person networking meetings may become infrequent connections when you leave the group.

You may build a networking database of 500 or 5,000 names, but you can't effectively interact with all of them; probably you can't remember who many of them are. It is a best practice to create a "touches plan" anticipating when and how you will connect with them for each of your "top of mind" contacts.

Worksheet 3.1 Creating a Top Contacts Group provides a sample of the kind of information you can track easily. [The form for you to use is found in Appendix 2, page 193.] By organizing your contacts' data in a one-table format you can see relationships among people that might be lost in the database.

Top Contacts Worksheet

Person's name, contact information	What person does, Company's industry or individual's demographic	How you met the person? How well you know the person	What is the basis of your close connection with the person?	How can you help this person?	How can this person help you?	Where/how will you connect with this person?	How do you define a successful relationship with this person?
Charlie Brown	Financial advisor, Company NAICS: 52211*	At Gotham City Networking group meeting	Shared clients Close colleagues Know him only in the context of work	Introduce him to my contacts and our shared client	Meet his contacts at our shared client	Make a lunch date with our shared client contacts	Expand our relationships with our shared client
Susan Smith	Corporate lawyer, Company NAICS: 54111	On the Boy Scout Board with you	Children the same age who enjoy scouting Friends	Share insights from my area of expertise with her	Introduce me to GC's who need my expertise	Dinner after the next board meeting	Become closer friends and help each other succeed
Add more rows as needed							

* https://www.census.gov/eos/www/naics/.

Sorting

Hopefully you will keep your contact information in some kind of sortable database—Outlook, Excel, or a Customer Relationship Management [CRM] program. If you are interested in purchasing a program, the American Bar Association's Legal Technology Resource Center publishes an annual legal technology buyer's guide.

In order to use your contacts list effectively, it is important to capture some key data so you can sort by different criteria depending on what you want to use the names for. For example, your holiday list will probably be different than your top referrers list and will be used for different purposes.

Begin with basic data categories such as current client, former client, referral source, friend, colleague, etc. Add other key data including the following:

- How you met the person
- Shared affiliations and groups
- Other groups they belong to
- Their work information—company/industry
- Their contact information
- Personal information—birthday, family members, hobbies
- Your connection follow-up notes—ten fields in which to note when, why, and how you contacted them after you met them
  - The first such "touch" is obviously the follow-up note after initially meeting them.
- Referrals to them or from them—to whom, when, for what reason
  - How the referrals worked out.

You may also want to add a rating field so that you can easily bring up your top 20 or 50 contacts all at once.[8] It is especially important to keep this field current so at the bottom of the field include an automatic "most recent update date" entry so that you will know when you last moved people on or off of these lists.

Creating the initial data sort can be a tedious chore, but once set up, you can easily slot all subsequent entries into the proper categories as you add them to your database. If you don't want to begin by annotating all contacts, start with those in Figure 3.4's top three categories: the handful, the top-of-mind 20 and the 50 focus lists.

To begin to populate your holiday card file turn to lists from the organizations you belong to, your alumni association, your current and former colleagues, and your personal friends and family list. If you are active on LinkedIn, be sure to cross-reference those names with your LinkedIn contacts list.

---

8. See Bill Jawitz, "Tapping the Hidden Gold in Your Contacts List," http://successtrackesq.com/successtips/tapping-the-hidden-gold-your-contacts-list/.

To keep the lists fresh and to enable you to review previous encounters, make it a habit to add names or add information to names already on the list after every networking activity. Two examples follow:

- At your monthly general networking group meeting you heard that your contact A was changing firms. After the meeting, update your database and make a point of sending the person a congratulatory note. Record your action and the reason for it in your database.
- After an event, add the names of the handful of people with whom you had meaningful conversations, making sure to add the specifics of where you met them, why they were there, and conversation highlights.

Periodically go through your list and winnow out names with dated information or names that slipped in even though you don't know them at all.

If this seems like a lot of work, it can be. For the ministerial parts you might want to hire an intern or part-time worker to do it for you. Often you can hire someone online who is skilled at data input. Of course, you will want to summarize conversations and add value judgments yourself.

The networkers I interviewed use their lists in various ways. For example,

Marc W. Halpert, a LinkedIn trainer, has a huge contacts database. He likens it to a bank because he "withdraws" people when he sees a way he can help them or they can help him. To support this role, he intentionally cultivates an extensive, diverse resources group.

James K. Landau, a lawyer, spends the first half hour of every day reviewing his contact management systems lists, key names, etc. He tracks activities in Outlook's folders and subfolders, and uses his daily review to determine where to expend his efforts.

Lenny Carraturo, commercial business development officer at Wells Fargo bank, tracks his interactions on an Excel spreadsheet noting those he meets with and those with whom he exchanges leads.

Martin S. Klein, a trust and estates lawyer, plans to see his top contacts face to face two or three times a year. In-between he keeps in touch via email or invitations to join him at various events.

Many others use their list for "keep in touch" activities such as newsletters, event invites, and the like.

Chapter Summary

Contacts are the raw material for your networking activities. You will want to take the time necessary to build out your three networks—personal, occupational, and aspirational. Then you will want to organize your total list around your goals and strategies and create action subgroups of 5, 20, and 50 contacts who will get primary attention during the next six months to a year.

Use your contacts proactively. "Make sure people know what you're interested in, and when you need something, ask. Adding value for your network members and allowing them to reciprocate will strengthen your network."[9] At the same time, take care to balance the weak links' access to diverse experiences with your strong links' psychosocial support.

In the next three chapters we will examine a variety of in-person organizations that provide opportunities for building and maintaining a network that is relevant to your goals.

9. Liane Davey, "Everyone's Network Should Provide Two Things," *Harvard Business Review*, September 30, 2016, https://hbr.org/2016/09/everyones-network-should-provide-two-things.

In-Person Networking Venues 4

Some networkers build all their relationships through organizations. Others may go to organized events but prefer to network by spending most of their time with individuals one-on-one. Certain people bypass already formed groups and create their own groups.[1]

Still, most people at some point in their career join groups. Their reasons vary according to where they are in their career and their networking skill level. Some of the primary reasons people look for and join groups are:

- To meet referral sources
- To meet potential clients
- To make new friends
- To stay top of mind with current important contacts
- To learn something new about a practice area, industry, geographic location, hobby, etc.
- To gain competitive intelligence
- To develop resources to use personally
- To develop resources to share with others

Finding a group is easy; just ask your colleagues what they belong to or run a Google search by location or industry or activity and hundreds of options will appear. But, *selecting* a group can be daunting because there are so many kinds of groups, associations, and organizations and so many entities within each category.

1. Although we often use the words "organization" and "group" as synonyms, in fact there is a difference. Both are formed around central themes or purposes, but groups tend to be less structured than organizations. For example, the American Bar Association is an organization with sections, divisions, and committees. A Meetup group of lawyers with a common goal but no real organizational framework would be a group.

I ran a Google search for my county, Westchester County, New York, and Google offered the following results:

- Networking groups in Westchester County, NY, yielded about 116,000 results.
- Westchester, NY, networking for professionals yielded 450,000 results.
- Business networking groups in Westchester County, NY, yielded 1,930,000 results.

Of course, Google searches include duplications and dead ends, but the sheer quantity does suggest the magnitude of the groups and organizations universe.

In this overview chapter we discuss why and how to choose one kind of group versus another, and review best practices for making the most of your time in any organization.

The universe of networking groups is so large and heterogenous that to simplify choices I have subdivided it into eight categories. These specific categories are discussed in Chapters 5 and 6.

- In Chapter 5 we will look at five kinds of in-person groups: general mixed membership groups, single profession groups, industry/trade associations, professional associations, and mastermind or peer advisor groups.
- In Chapter 6 we will discuss three kinds of in-person groups, all of which require members to be invited to join: personal private groups; honorary societies; and social, philanthropic, cultural, religious, and civic nonprofits.
- The summary for Chapters 4, 5, and 6 is at the end of Chapter 6.

Eight Categories of In-Person Networking Groups

General Mixed Membership Groups

Single Profession Groups

Industry/Trade Associations

Professional Associations

Peer Advisor Groups

Personal Private Groups

Honorary Societies

Social/Philanthropic/Cultural/Religious/Civic Nonprofits

The Universe of Organizations

For the purpose of business development, the organization universe can be segmented into eight broad categories:

- **General mixed membership groups**, such as BNI, Gotham City Networking, American Business Associates [aba], which usually include a wide variety of occupations
- **Single profession groups** such as The Attorney Roundtable; INBLF[2] and Primerus
- **Industry/trade associations**, such as Associated Builders & Contractors [ABC] and American Bankers Association [ABA], geared to specific occupations, industries, and trades
- **Professional associations**, such as the American Bar Association [ABA] and the Association of International Certified Professional Accountants [AICPA], where people with the same specialized background go for education and networking
- **Mastermind or peer advisor groups**, such as Vistage, Network! Network!, and Collaberex LLC, which combine networking and peer counseling
- **Personal private groups**, that is, private groups set up by one individual to further his/her own networking capabilities through regular interactions with a trusted group of close colleagues and friends.
- **Honorary societies** and groups where membership is by invitation, such as the College of Commercial Arbitrators and the Litigation Counsel of America
- **Social, philanthropic, cultural, religious, and civic nonprofits**, such as United Way, Savvy Ladies, YMCA, and League of Women Voters

Selecting the Best Organizations for You

By now you've figured out that there are too many options. How do you choose one or two? Go back again to the research part of your goal setting and review what you've learned about where the people you want to meet go for information, advice, and resources.

- What are the major groups and organizations where they congregate?
- Where do they go for trusted information, advice, and resources?
- Are any of them open to vendors, people who work with an industry or trade group but do not practice the trade?

2. INBLF stands for International Network of Boutique & Independent Law Firms.

- Do they have local chapters?
- Do they have entities in other geographic areas that are important to you?

Think about your target market when deciding who you want to meet: referrers or potential clients, or resource people, or some combination.

- What mix will be most beneficial for you in terms of your goals?
- Do you want a general group that includes people with Business-to-Business [B2B] and Business-to-Consumer [B2C] businesses or would you prefer a group composed of just one or the other?
- Will the members of the group you select be able to open the doors you want opened?

Jonathan Rosen, founder of Collaberex, says, "People do business with people who provide the most value and who they also know, like, and trust . . .You should only network with others who are most likely to be able to provide each other the most value, then work hard to create relationships with those people to get to know them, like them, and trust them."

You might want to review your career goals and create a networking strategy focused on getting to know more people in your own profession. You might want to make friends with others who do what you do or look for more senior practitioners who can help you grow professionally. Or grow a reputation and career through service in your professional association.

Networking can help you obtain the visibility and contacts to develop a client base or enhance your career, but equally important is its ability to make you feel acknowledged and valued. "There is a basic human need to feel a sense of belonging, to be part of something bigger than ourselves and have a place where we contribute and feel valued. We all need to feel connected to others."[3]

Most groups will encourage you to visit before you buy either by comp'ing your first few visits or offering a discount price. Use the opportunity to get a sense of the group.

- Do you like the people at the meetings?
- Do you like their programs?
- Do they focus on issues and activities that are relevant to you?
- Do you like the culture?
- Do they seem to share contacts and resources?
- Does the room feel warm and personal or cool and clique-y?
- Do the members share your values and goals?
- Did you meet anyone you would like to see again?

3. Susan G. Parker, "Are You Ready to Get Serious About Networking?" Harvard Management Communications Letter, February 2003, pp. 9–10.

Joining a group is a commitment, so ask what rules and expectations govern the group.

- What are the attendance and participation requirements?
- Are efforts to help others measured? If so, how are they measured? Are there leads or referral quotas?
- What are the demographic requirements for membership in terms of age, geographic location, race, gender, and, of course, business categories?
- How strictly do they enforce the rules? Are people kicked out for infractions?
- How long do most members remain active in the group?

Most of the interviewees belong to a variety of groups, which, like a patchwork quilt, offer different kinds of members and advance different goals, but taken as a whole reflect their strategic networking plans.[4] For example,

- A corporate lawyer with a large merger and acquisitions practice is a director on boards related to his practice area and on boards related to industries his clients are in.
- A litigator interested in referrals from lawyers belongs to half a dozen bar associations and to two general networking groups composed of lawyers and business executives.
- A banker interested in acquiring companies as bank clients belongs to a Westchester County government financial advisory board and the boards of several well-known nonprofits, and is an active member of several mixed membership networking groups.
- A rainmaking managing partner bases his networking in two small, personal groups.
- The COO of an alternative energy company belongs to half a dozen groups where her clients and colleagues are, and to several gender-specific networking groups.

In each instance the networker is allotting his/her time and energy to groups that offer relationships and knowledge important to his/her business growth goals.

Best Practices for Maximizing Your Group Time

Don't join a group unless you are willing to make a commitment to participate. Paper members—those who pay dues but rarely show up for any activity—seldom share in the benefits of group networking. To move toward your goals through groups you have to implement your commitment:

4. Information from their LinkedIn profiles, website profiles, personal interviews.

- Calendar meeting dates.
- Offer to help. Join a committee, participate in a program, plan the annual party. In the smaller subgroups you will get to know people more intimately.
- Get to know members at one-on-ones between meetings. In one-on-one meetings you can begin to really know a person and what is important to him/her.

You also want some visibility within the group. To become a visible, active member of your group, take on leadership positions, introduce new members to the group, or produce content for the group. Take advantage of the opportunities offered.

Marcia Golden belongs to organizations because she is a "face to face" shy person. She likes the fact that the regularity of group meetings holds people accountable for follow-up. She, too, believes that it is important to take leadership positions in groups and finds that having such a position is an effective tool that forces her to be social.

As Stacy Francis, CEO of Francis Financial, put it: "It is better to be in the front of the room than the back. If you are not the group founder, then seek a speaking opportunity or a leadership role. This kind of visibility creates trust within the group because the position has credibility built into it."

The Life Cycle of Group Involvement

Despite the fact that some people stay in organizations for many years, there is a typical life cycle for active group participation. As Figure 4.1 shows, you join an organization and initially just go to meetings and events while you "get your sea legs" and figure out where you want to spend your time. Then you agree to join a committee or take on a leadership position. You move up and through leadership positions and after president emeritus you are back to attending meetings and events.

Some organizations have specific rules regarding time allowed for specific positions; in others, passage through active member positions is run according to unwritten norms. Whatever the rules, when you join a group you should understand the time span of available opportunities so that you can maximize your use of these opportunities and accommodate the group's time demands in your schedule. Many groups record attendance and penalize members who miss too many meetings.

Figure 4.1 Working Your Way through Organizations

Involvement takes time. So how many groups should you join and how should you evaluate the benefits? Typically, experienced networkers are active in only one or two groups because of the time commitments. They may go to other groups' events or show up periodically at other group meetings, but they know it is more effective to concentrate their efforts.

On average, people stay in a group for three to five years. Westchester Business Network [WBN] is an exception to the three-year rule. Some of the original group members are still active 30 years later. Approximately one-third of the current members have been in WBN for at least ten years. Occasionally they refer each other for work-related purposes, but the main attraction for the long-timers are friendships and access to very diverse resources that have developed through friendships made and maintained over the years.

Marc W. Halpert doesn't really like groups because he feels that there is insufficient one-on-one time. Yet, he belongs to four groups at the moment. He says, "You give until you don't need to and when you can't give any more you drop out."

The length of a person's membership in any specific group is also influenced by his or her career needs. You may need to move to a different kind of group because you are on a different rung of your career ladder or have new responsibilities. Perhaps you were creating a referral base that is now well established, so now you want to join a group where you can gain additional knowledge or find additional resources.

Sometimes general-purpose groups continue for years with the same leadership, similar membership, and similar group goals. Other times they morph into different configurations with different names, different leadership, and different members. Marcia R. Golden, President of DJD Golden, a marketing company, explained the transformation sequence for a group she joined in the 1980s. As she tells it, she joined the Metropolitan Business Network [MBN] and served on its steering committee. Five years after joining, the group had a leadership shake-up and Marcia left.

She called two friends and said, "Let's start a networking group." They began a group with eight people; a decade later it had 30 members. The group functioned just as MBN had. Originally called The Breakfast Club, the name changed several times over the years both to suit fashions in networking and to reflect changes in leadership and membership.

- The Breakfast Club [TBC] name began to sound too light and trite. Several years later, with new leadership, the name was changed to Business Development Network [BDN] to emphasize the purpose of the group and because they thought that the previous name sounded too informal.
- Then the word "networking" began to have negative connotations, so the name was changed to NY Business Forum [NYBF]. The same core group of people saw the group through all these name changes.
- Today, Westchester Business Network [WBN][5] is the primary surviving group. This group was founded by David Rosenberg, an IT consultant, who lived in Westchester as a Westchester-based group. Those original members who lived in the county joined WBN.

Whatever the reason, the old chapter has run its course. You have moved up and off the leadership trail. Your friends will stay friends, and you have gotten what you joined for. Once your current groups have grown stale, it is time to evaluate the experience and return to the reasons you joined.

- Have the reasons been met?
- If not, why not? Is there something you can do to get more out of the group?
- If yes, your goals for this group have been met, it may be time to move on. So, go back to your planning documents and goals to decide how to change your networking strategy.

---

5. Profiled in Chapter 5.

Chapter Summary

In this chapter we discussed various kinds of in-person organizations and reasons why you might select one kind rather than another. We also discussed the advantages of participation in whatever group you join and looked at the active participation cycle. In the next two chapters we will talk about each of the eight organization categories in more detail.

In-Person Groups 5

In this chapter we will look at general networking groups. Some groups combine business and professional members, others only members of the same profession. Some include only business to business enterprises [B2B], others only business to consumer enterprises [B2C], and some want members representing a broad spectrum of B2B and B2C occupations. Usually a group will lean toward one category more than another. In most of these groups, you can join if there is space for someone with your business or professional focus.

The groups addressed in this chapter are

- General mixed membership
- Single profession
- Industry/trade associations
- Professional associations
- Mastermind or peer advisor

To make the differentiations among specific groups clearer we include examples that highlight each category's primary characteristics and some of the reasons why people join each type of group. Table 5.1 summarizes the basic characteristics of the specific groups we will profile in this chapter.

Table 5.1 Groups Profiled in This Chapter

Name, Year Founded	Group Category	Geographic Scope	Meeting Frequency, Size	Program	Member Criteria, Website URL
American Business Associates [ABA] 1988	General mixed membership networking group	Metro NYC	Twice a month; 13 groups each with 20 to 40 members	Structured by facilitator	"Owners, senior managers, and senior sales executives of small to medium size businesses operating in the NY metro area marketplace" one person per category http://www.aba-ny.com
Attorney Roundtable [ART] 2000	Lawyer-only membership networking group	Local, Long Island, NY	Monthly; 20 to 25 members	Loosely structured	"Essentially a loose affiliation of solo and small firm niche practice lawyers" two people per category http://attorneyrt.com/ART
Business Networking International [BNI] 1985	General mixed membership networking group	International, 220,000 members, 8,399 chapters	Weekly; Chapters range from 20 to 100 people	Very structured	Broad spectrum of professionals and business people, both B2B and B2C one person per category

Name, Year Founded	Group Category	Geographic Scope	Meeting Frequency, Size	Program	Member Criteria, Website URL
Collaberex 2016	Target market focused, mixed membership networking group	Metro NYC	Monthly; 15 to 20 members per group	Structured by facilitator	Noncompeting professionals and business executives who prospect in the same target market one person per category https://collaberex.com/
Gotham City Networking Inc. 1997	General mixed membership networking group	Mostly Metro NYC and several other cities	Every six weeks; 29 groups, 10 to 25 members per group	Structured	Business professionals and service-oriented professionals in complementary fields, usually one person per category, but several groups are "noncompete" so anyone can join http://www.gothamnetworking.com/ private group listserv
International Network of Boutique & Independent Law Firms [INBLF] 2004	Lawyer only membership networking group	International	Monthly; 25 to 50 members per group	Loosely structured	"An invitation-only group of lawyers in boutique firms who represent the highest level of knowledge, experience and reputation" one person per category https://www.inblf.com/

continued

Name, Year Founded	Group Category	Geographic Scope	Meeting Frequency, Size	Program	Member Criteria, Website URL
The International Society of Primerus Law Firms 1992	Independent boutique law firms, lawyers	International, 40 countries, 130 cities	Annual global conference; regional and practice group meetings	Structured by association staff	"We seek out, accept and retain only the best firms for membership. Each firm is screened to ensure its commitment to excellence as embodied in the Six Pillars: Integrity, Excellent Work Product, Reasonable Fees, Continuing Legal Education, Civility and Community Service."
Vistage 1967	CEOs/business executives, professionals	International	Monthly; 12 to 16 members per group	Structured by facilitator	Private "peer advisory boards" of high-caliber CEOs, top executives, small business leaders, or professional service advisors https://www.vistage.com
Westchester Business Network [WBN] 1989	General B2B mixed membership networking group	Local—Westchester County, NY	Monthly; 15 to 35 members	Loosely structured	Various professionals and B2B business people, one person per category no website, has private group listserv

Let's turn to an examination of each of the five categories discussed in this chapter.

General Mixed Membership Groups

General mixed membership groups fit Co-Managing Partner Larry Hutcher's description of a group: "A networking group is like a mall. You need strong anchor tenants and then small guys in-between." For this reason, many general purpose, mixed groups are built around a "real estate" core usually consisting of commercial and residential real estate brokers, local bankers, real estate lawyers, accountants, mortgage brokers, title agencies, insurance agents, and marketing agency people who often work together outside the group and so form a cohesive base within a larger, more amorphous group.

These groups usually have either

- B2B only members, or
- B2B and B2C members.

All general membership groups have membership guidelines covering guests, the membership application process, attendance requirements, election of board of directors, and so on.

Usually, general membership groups allow only one member per business category; but in order to have a sufficiently large membership, many groups allow members to represent a narrow slice of their business capabilities. So, for example, a marketing and PR agency member may represent only the online PR services for the purposes of the group while other people take the marketing, traditional PR, and video slots. A trust and estates and tax law attorney usually will represent one or the other practice focus.

Most of these groups are volunteer led. They are either run by a single individual, usually the group founder, or a small executive committee, sometimes appointed and sometimes elected by the group members. The leadership sets the criteria for membership, fees, member participation guidelines, and program content.

Standard general membership group programs include the following activities:

- A general networking period before the meeting begins
- Introductions: one-minute elevator speeches
    - Longer introductions of visiting people who are considering joining the group
- Thank yous and leads wanted
- A program component:

    - A spotlight presentation by a member of the group
    - A presentation by an outside expert
    - Group discussion of a single topic: sometimes as a whole group, often by table
- Reminder to meet with group members one-on-one or in small groups between meetings
- End-of-meeting networking, often setting one-on-one dates

Groups meet regularly, but the amount of time between meetings varies. Some meet weekly, others monthly, semimonthly or every six weeks, often for breakfast or lunch. Meetings usually last approximately two hours. Cost varies widely. Some very informal groups charge no fee; members meet at a restaurant and are responsible for their own check. Usually there is a membership fee that covers meeting room costs, food, and, for those with an administration component, funds to cover the cost of running the organization. Dues range from several hundred dollars up to $10,000 a year.

Most groups have participation requirements, often stated in explicit detail. The following are taken from the Attorney Round Table website:

- Clear commitment to participate actively in the Attorney Round Table: regular attendance at meetings and events, with an aspirational goal of missing no more than two meetings each year (i.e., attendance at 9 of the 11 monthly meetings annually)
- RSVPing promptly by e-mail in advance regarding attendance at meetings
- Service on a committee and other appropriate functions
- Interaction with other attorney round table members in between meetings
- Bringing to the group at least one new visitor (qualified prospective member) per year
- Remaining current with timely payment of semi-annual dues and any assessments.[1]

All general membership networking groups say they provide resources, ideas, and business opportunities for each other. These groups are also similar in terms of program content. Yet the groups themselves are each different. They each have their own mission, purpose, and areas of emphasis. Group cultures vary widely and give each group its own character and personality. The

1. ART website, attorneyrt.com.

American Business Associates' core values listed in Sidebar 5.1 capture the basic principles of most successful networking groups.

Sidebar 5.1 American Business Associates Group's Core Values

- *Authenticity: We believe in realistic, "down to earth" interactions that produce results for our clients.*
- *Consideration: We believe that productive interactions are best initiated and maintained by individuals who are considerate and respectful of each other.*
- *Generosity: Quite simply, we believe that one must give to get. The spirit of cooperation creates a win-win attitude in business as well as life.*
- *Communication: We believe that the continuity of any relationship is a function of open-ended dialog.*
- *Being Strong, Yet Flexible: We are strong on our core values yet flexible on the means to uphold our core values.*
- *Longevity: We believe in long-term mutually beneficial relationships.*
- *Confidentiality: We honor and respect information which is given in a sensitive or confidential manner.*[2]

When choosing a group, it is important to attend one or two meetings as a guest to make sure you are comfortable with its mission and the culture as expressed by the members at meetings. For example, let's compare Business Networking International [BNI] and Westchester Business Network [WBN], two groups that interpret the "give not get" philosophy in very different ways.

Business Networking International

BNI is one of the "any business person can join" groups, but only one person to a business category. It may include professionals, contractors, spa owners and hairdressers, as well as a multitude of doctors and lawyers representing their own specific areas of practice.

"The mission of BNI is to help members increase their business through a structured, positive and professional referral marketing program that enables them to develop meaningful, long-term relationships with quality business professionals."[3]

Its mantra is: "It's simple, Givers Gain®. That's all there is to it. Once you've joined, the giving and receiving begins and you'll start to see your business

2. ABA website, http://www.aba-ny.com/resources/index.php.
3. All quotes about the BNI structure are from the website, https://www.bni.com/about/history.

grow." Their site says that within the last 12 months they have had "10.1 M Member Referrals and $ 14.3 B Member Closed Business."[4]

BNI chapters meet weekly, usually for breakfast beginning at 7 a.m. Their programs are highly structured with an emphasis on leads wanted and given, and closed new business. Many novice networkers begin in BNI groups because they are locally based and the strictly followed meeting agenda helps them to learn the ropes of networking.

Approximately one-third of the networkers interviewed did or do participate in BNI groups. Those who like the group reference the meeting structure and appreciate it's focus on leads.

Stacy Francis, a financial planner, leads her BNI group of 80 people. She likes it because "it teaches you how to network, helps me create stories to explain my business, creates discipline because I am reminded weekly of the need to grow my business."

Stacy estimates that one-quarter of her referrals come from her BNI colleagues.

Alla Roytberg, a lawyer, likes the mandated structure, the attendance requirement, the one-minute introductions, and the statistics regarding leads given and received. She has gotten work from members of her chapter.

Marcia Sloman, a professional organizer, and Vik Rajan, a social networking entrepreneur, both were in BNI chapters for three years. Each one joined to get business and so appreciated the competitive focus on leads and referrals.

Those who don't like BNI, like Marc Halpert, take issue with the focus on quantity of leads instead of lead quality.

Westchester Business Network

WBN is another local general membership group. Its culture is grounded in the long-term friendships among many members who have been in the group for a decade or more. The group's Statement of Purpose focuses on referrals:

> The Westchester Business Network is a member-owned, member-operated, not-for-profit organization which exists solely for the purpose of developing relationships which result in generating leads, referrals, introductions and business for its members. . . . The premise is that if everyone is bringing business into the room, ultimately everyone will get leads and business out of the room.[5]

4. BNI website, May 16, 2018, https://www.bni.com/why-join.
5. WBN, "Statement of Purpose," undated [emphasis added].

This sounds very similar to BNI's purpose but in practice it is very different. There are no BNI-like lead quotas and emphasis on bringing in business. David Rosenbaum begins each meeting by saying, "We exist for the purpose of introductions, meaningful connections and ultimately money in our pockets." The culture is laid back and informal. Meetings have a clublike, friendly, banter-filled atmosphere. The group emphasizes creation of deep relationships that should, and often do, lead to shared resources, referrals, and business.

> We don't sell to each other, but we can buy from each other.

Midway between these approaches, but nearer to WBN is Gotham City Networking Inc., called Gotham by its members.

Gotham City Networking Inc.

Gotham leadership encourages what they call a "tribal networking" feeling and speak of the "family" of members helping each other in the spirit of friendship and mutual growth. Gotham's collaborations are guided by its Mission Statement and networking philosophy:

> **Their mantra: It's Better to Give Than Receive, But What Goes Around, Comes Around.™**
>
> Tribal Networking: To forge business relationships steeped in the spirit of community that go beyond matters of immediate concern. This spirit is best served by fostering a climate characterized by our mantra. We become non-salaried, non-commissioned sales people for each other through the relationships we build.
>
> At Gotham, we seek to create a family, or we like to say tribal, environment stimulating business growth along with enriched social, creative, intellectual, artistic, and charitable experiences. We bring together service-oriented professionals in complementary fields to share contacts, ideas and resources and endeavor to enrich each participant through acts undertaken with a genuine concern for the welfare of our fellow networkers and the world.
>
> We are business networking with a social conscience.[6]

6. Gotham City Networking's Mission Statement was provided by Nancy Schess, one of the group's founders.

Gotham chapters and group-wide activities reinforce the tribal notion. There are not only local geographic chapters, there are also chapters for lefties, sustainable business, nonprofits, and health care. In addition, the group sponsors events that any member may go to, including cocktail parties, casual drinks get togethers, a film festival, softball team, and "battle of the bands" competition. Members are also encouraged to "ride the circuit," meaning attend meetings of groups other than your own.

American Business Associates [ABA]

"ABA is New York Metro's premier business development and networking association dedicated to helping small to mid-sized businesses dramatically increase sales by providing dynamic business connections and superior resources. ABA is the longest running professionally managed group in the metro New York area for B2B Networking."[6] Meetings are led by experienced facilitators, who run the groups as a business.[7]

ABA is similar to other general membership groups in terms of its composition, mission, and so on. However, it differs from the other three because it is run by an owner-facilitator who adds an educational focus to the meetings. Discussing the role of the professional owner-facilitator, Ellen Volpe said: "Energy is the key to group leadership. It takes lots of work to keep groups viable and fresh. I have a process. I know what agendas should be."

Her groups are not mastermind groups; rather she plans and leads discussions built around what she observes people in each group need. In her groups she creates an environment in which members feel comfortable practicing new behaviors. The purpose of the councils [groups] is "to learn about others, leverage the connections."[8]

Ellen explains the groups' membership as people with "long reach but no frequency." Because her groups meet twice a month, she creates that continuity for the members. She says that "One person with connections will soon hit diminishing returns. But, when you are in a group built around many people with strong networks, with whom you develop relationships, opportunities multiply."

6. Quotes in sidebar box and here are from ABA website, http://www.aba-ny.com/inside/index.php.

7. Other groups organized or run by paid professionals include Vistage, Collaborex, Network! Network! and many others.

8. Greenwald notes from October 12, 2017, meeting of the ABA Roosevelt Council.

"The essence and foundation of the ABA technique is to build rapport and trust between members for the purpose of leveraging each other's contacts and connections, and for the further purpose of expanding each of their businesses. The ABA atmosphere and technique is by nature entrepreneurial. It is not bureaucratic or corporate."[9]

As with other groups, the emphasis is on getting to know about each other and each other's business so you can make and receive appropriate introductions. The focus of this group is connections. "We don't care what you do; we want to know who you know," says Volpe.

> Ellen Volpe, ABA's owner-facilitator, says that 'in today's environment networking has become transactional—card exchanges. Without frequent in-person meetings energy dissipates. You need energy to stay in touch today. You need to get a person's undivided attention.'

Reasons to Join General Mixed Membership Groups

People join general mixed membership groups for a variety of reasons.

- When you are building a network joining these groups can be a quick way to identify and interact with a variety of individuals in different occupations and professions.
- For many people the main purpose is to develop relationships that help them grow their business. Often these people become close friends, part of their strong links, personal contacts.
- Others want to learn from the variety of members with different capabilities and different approaches to important issues.
- The range of occupations in these groups creates a multifaceted resource network that can be useful for individual members and their circle of contacts.

Members often stay in general membership groups past the time when it is valuable as a work-related resource because the time demands are minimal since they know everyone, and they enjoy the camaraderie of their networking friends. They appreciate and learn from the conversations even if actual business opportunities decrease over time.

9. ABA website, http://www.aba-ny.com/inside/index.php.

Marcia Sloman, a professional organizer, has been in Westchester Business Network since its beginning in 1989. Asked why she stays, she replied: "We are smart, sincere, all in one room and resources for each other. And, sometimes we get business from each other."

Single Profession/Vetted Professionals Networking Groups

Single profession groups are similar to general mixed membership groups in terms of the group's objectives and the way they are run; but unlike general membership groups their membership is limited to one profession.

The founders of such groups usually create them to fill a need related to their own networking strategy. For example, when David Abeshouse left his law firm and went out on his own, he and an accountant friend created the Attorney Roundtable [ART] because he felt that he needed an equivalent of the complementary resources and collegiality he had in the law firm.

We profile three groups each representing a version of the single profession idea: the Attorney Roundtable [ART], the equivalent of the resources in a full service firm; the International Network of Boutique & Independent Law Firms [INBLF], a selection of highly credentialed lawyers; and Primerus, an international affiliation of independent boutique law firms.

The Attorney Roundtable

The website defines ART as "[A] lawyers' business networking group comprised of some of the leading practitioners in their respective areas of law practice in the New York metropolitan area."[10] ART's strict membership criteria ensure that the group will be a useful forum for information, referrals, and collaboration. The membership criteria include the following:

- Well-defined principal substantive area of law practice for experienced practicing attorneys [at least seven years]
- Focus or concentration in that one niche area, greater than 50 percent of individual's practice and that of firm
- No more than two members per law practice area in the group ("Noah's Ark" competitive model: two-by-two)
- Ownership of practice/owner-officer-senior manager of corporation
- Located in one local geographic area [metro NY]

10. ART website home page, https://www.attorneyrt.com/.

- If any ART member subsequently joins a multi-practice firm or otherwise effects a change in practice that does not qualify under ART guidelines, that member's participation in ART is subject to immediate termination by the Executive Committee.[11]

In other respects, ART operates in the same manner as general mixed membership groups.

David's testimonial on ART's website attests to the value of the group:

"Although ART is . . . essentially a loose affiliation of niche practice lawyers, it has served for me and other solos and small firm lawyers as a substitute for having a larger firm with many partners in different areas of practice, without many of the attendant hassles.

"We reap the benefits through strong mutual support from friends and colleagues . . . assisting each other by discussing issues of law practice management, referring clients to members in other niche areas of practice, providing information about our areas of expertise to those practicing in other niches when issues arise in their practices, working together on appropriate matters, and in just about every other legitimate way imaginable."[12]

The International Network of Boutique & Independent Law Firms

The International Network of Boutique & Independent Law Firms [INBLF][13] is another kind of one profession/one kind of firm group created because its founder, Steven Spielvogel, when he left his AmLaw 100 firm, wanted to be able to refer work to lawyers of a similar caliber to those in his former firm. He created a network of highly credentialed lawyers for this explicit purpose.

When Steven joined a small business litigation boutique firm he realized that when opportunities arose in other legal areas he had three choices:

- offer nothing, just say we don't do that, which seemed very unsatisfactory;
- refer out to friends at full-service law firms and worry that his client might be poached; or
- refer out to other top credentialed lawyers in other boutique firms.

---

11. Adapted from language on the ART website, http://attorneyrt.com/ART_Guidelines_Application.html.

12. David J. Abeshouse, quote from the ART website, http://www.attorneyrt.com/ART_Testimonials.html.

13. The International Network of Boutique Firms is now called the International Network of Boutique & Independent Law Firms, but is still using the original initials.

Option 3 seemed the most viable if he could find lawyers of the same quality as those at his former firm, Sullivan & Cromwell.

"When I carried a Sullivan & Cromwell litigation bag and it said S&C on it, it was a rebuttable presumption that you were an amazing and brilliant lawyer. I am hoping that the INBLF imprimatur will similarly create a rebuttable presumption for all INBLF-approved attorneys."[14]

Steven found members for his initial chapter by lunching with lawyers with prestigious resumes in boutique firms. He focused on each attorney's c.v.—schools, clerkships, honors, publications, and legal community leadership. Once he had secured a dozen "yeses" he held a get acquainted party, and when that went well, the group began its current format of monthly meetings.

Soon he was crisscrossing the country interviewing highly credentialed attorneys in boutique firms in major markets and forming new chapters. Once a national network of credentialed lawyers was in place, Steven began to add full-service international firms. Today there are hundreds of member firms in over 40 commercial centers in the United States and Canada, plus 39 other countries around the world.

Despite its growth, the membership criteria remains the same: "To assemble a network of preeminent boutique law firms in a wide array of practice fields and to ensure a uniform level of excellence by inviting only the highest quality single-discipline law firms to join the INBLF."[15]

The International Society of Primerus Law Firms

Another version of single industry networking groups is the affiliated firm group whose members act as resources and provide referral opportunities for each other. One of these is Primerus, the law firm group that the Barton LLP law firm belongs to. Roger E. Barton, firm managing partner, attends many of Primerus' conferences in order to meet local lawyers from other geographic areas who serve as both referrers for his firm and resources for his clients.

The Primerus website defines them as:

> Primerus is a society of the world's finest independent, boutique law firms. . . . Primerus provides clients easy access to the right lawyer, with the right skills, in the right location, and at the right cost. We seek

14. Quoted in Karen Donovan, "Some Small Law Firms Find Strength in Numbers," *The New York Times*, June 8, 2007, https://www.nytimes.com/2007/06/08/business/08law.html.
15. INBLF website, https://www.inblf.com.

out, accept and retain only the best firms for membership. Each firm is screened to ensure its commitment to excellence as embodied in the Six Pillars: Integrity, Excellent Work Product, Reasonable Fees, Continuing Legal Education, Civility and Community Service.[16]

Reasons to Join Single Profession Groups of Vetted Professionals

Especially for professionals in boutique firms or for solo practitioners, a group of vetted complementary professionals offers the advantage of "known quantities." Because they have met the group's membership criteria their relationships can begin at the "warm" contacts stage. As they interact at events and meetings, the members become trusted colleagues.

For the individual professional this kind of group offers several important advantages:

- Referral opportunities to trusted colleagues in other practice areas
- Learning opportunities from colleagues in similar situations but different practice areas
- Resources for the member and others in his circle of contacts
- Friendship

Industry/Trade Associations

Trade associations, also known as industry groups or associations, are founded and funded by and for the businesses or businesspeople in a specific industry or trade. Examples include:[17]

- Million Dollar Roundtable
- Chamber of Commerce
- International Council of Shopping Centers
- Solar Energy Industries Association
- Mortgage Bankers Association
- Biotechnology Industry Association
- Automobile Manufacturers Association

Membership is usually limited to individuals and/or companies in the specific industry or trade. Some organizations offer affiliate memberships as a source of revenue. Affiliate members are those who work with and for entities or individuals in the association. Some associations are nonprofit entities governed by a board of directors; others are run as businesses.

16. International Society of Primerus Law Firms, http://www.primerus.com/about.htm.
17. To find trade, industry, or professional associations use Google or Wikipedia.

Industry/trade groups typically engage in advertising; education; political activities; publishing; and a variety of local, state, and/or national meetings. They offer a chance for members of the industry or trade to work together on issues and in committees. They are a primary conduit for issue-related conversations, education, and activities such as lobbying, conferences, forums.

Reasons to Join Industry or Trade Groups

Professionals, as service providers to the trade or industry, use the opportunity to become visible in the industry and strengthen relationships with current clients and potential clients. It is a way to move from outside resource to insider status as a colleague on program committees, a speaker at conferences, and a contributor to association materials.

Professional firms can avail themselves of sponsorship opportunities that typically include visibility choices such as your name on the conference invitation, your name in the conference book, your name at the session or activity you sponsor. Sponsors at some conventions may participate in exclusive events where they can mingle with the organization's leaders or showcase their expertise on a panel. Conventions offer trade show opportunities where vendors can showcase their wares.

For affiliate members, participation in trade groups supplies an education in what's important to their target niche and why. It provides an opportunity to observe what information and opportunities they value; and learn the language they use to discuss their choices.

On the ABA Solosez listserv, a member answered a question about where to network by suggesting industry associations as fertile marketing territory:

Do you have a preferred client industry? If so, consider finding out if their trade association has an open membership policy. For example, I work with lots of graphic designers and advertising companies. I joined AIGA and the Ad Federation of America and became active, going to events, learning about the members and what they do and the industries in general. About 20 percent of my current business has come through those interactions either as direct business or from referrals. It takes time, it took me about 8 months before I got my first substantial client. But I had learned so much that I was able to speak and understand their language.[18]

18. Matthew Johnston, ABA Solosez Listserv, July 20, 2017.

Professional Associations

Professional associations are usually nonprofit groups that provide oversight of a profession, continuing education, and activities in the public interest. Representative groups include:

- American Bar Association [ABA]
- Association of International Certified Professional Accountants [AICPA]
- Association of Information Technology Professionals [AITP]
- Institute of Electrical and Electronics Engineers [IEEE]
- International Association of Business Communicators [IABC]

These groups offer members peer-to-peer interactions on committees, at continuing education classes, and at various events. Individuals join these groups to be able to grow their professional credentials and render service to their profession.

For example,

- Jessica Thaler-Parker is active on NYS Bar Association committees where she routinely moves up the responsibility ladder to chairperson because colleagues know that she will get things done. She doesn't need to tell people that she is an excellent project manager, because she demonstrates those skills by achieving committee goals.
- James K. Landau, a litigator interested in referrals from lawyers, holds leadership and committee positions in six bar associations. In this way he meets and becomes friends with attorneys who can send him work. He also belongs to two peer-to-peer general networking groups that include a number of professionals as well as potential clients.

> "Jessica attributes her NYSBA committee leadership appointments to her ability 'to get s___ done.'"

Linda A. Klein, past president of the American Bar Association (ABA), offers a textbook perfect example of someone who built a client base and a personal reputation through bar association activities. [See Figure 5.1.] As she tells it, as a young lawyer in a strange city she entered bar service to make friends.

She was soon appointed to the Governing Board of the Young Lawyers Division of her local bar association. As a new member "she got the job nobody wanted," to write an article on court rules changes. Her article in the *Atlanta Lawyer* magazine caught the eye of the chair of the State Bar Committee on Rules. He became her mentor.

Figure 5.1 Trajectory of Linda Klein's Ascent to ABA President

When he decided not to run for another term on the Board of Governors he offered her his seat. She ran an old-fashioned endorsement campaign and won. Two years later she ran for the executive committee of the Board of Governors and again won. Then it was her turn to run for an officer position. Again, in a contested election she won.

In 2003–2004 she began her ascent through the ABA leadership hierarchy by becoming chair of the Tort Trial and Insurance Practice Section. Key positions as she moved from section chair to ABA president included House of Delegates Committees [2004–2008], Chair of the House of Delegates [2010–2012], ABA Board of Governors [2012–current], President-Elect [2015–2016], President [2016–2017].[19]

> As Linda says, 'Networking is a two-way street. You are becoming part of a community. You have to want to be there and be willing to give to the success of the community.'

She attributes her continuing rise through each of these associations to the fact that she developed a reputation as a hard worker. "Other people saw leadership qualities in me. The harder I worked, the luckier I got." She also gained what she originally joined her local bar for—friends. Through these friends she obtains clients and work for her firm.

Reasons to Join Professional Associations

In the networking context, professional associations are useful venues for those who seek referrals from others in their profession. Typically, referrals occur when:

19. Baker Donelson website, her bio page, https://www.bakerdonelson.com/Linda-A-Klein.

- The referring professional is conflicted—and so cannot take the new client.
- The case is either too large or too small given the guidelines of the referrer's firm.
- The referrer has personal reasons for not wanting to take the case.
- The professional's client needs expertise that the professional doesn't have; so this work is given to someone trusted to treat the case as well as the professional would and to not steal the client from her/him.

Younger professionals can use the committee membership opportunity to meet and create relationships with senior people in their own field. Those in boutique firms or solo practice may use a professional association's activities as a forum to meet people in complementary areas who become part of their referral or resource network. People new to networking or fearful about networking often are comfortable meeting people in their professional associations because they feel comfortable with the culture and jargon of the group.

Mastermind Groups or Peer Advisor Groups

The mastermind concept is attributed to Napoleon Hill. In the early 20th century, he defined the main principle of such a group as "The coordination of knowledge and effort of two or more people who work toward a definite purpose, in the spirit of harmony."[20] The groups' activities are built around the principle of collaborative intelligence. Hill said, "No two minds ever come together without thereby creating a third invisible intangible force which may be likened to a third mind [the master mind]."[21]

Actually, Napoleon Hill's idea was not new. In 1727, Benjamin Franklin established the first such networking group—The Junto. It had a dozen members who met for mutual improvement—the first mastermind style group. Today there are many versions of mastermind groups—some with a focus on individual development and others usually categorized as peer-to-peer groups that add a business development component. We will look at an example of each kind of group.

20. Quoted in "What Is a Mastermind Group? A Definition—Blog, Tutorials" https://www.thesuccessalliance.com/what-is-a-mastermind-group/
21. Ibid.

Vistage

"Vistage, the world's leading business advisory and executive coaching organization"[22] is a mastermind style group focused on individual growth. Vistage offers six kinds of groups:

- Groups of professional service advisors in companies/firms with revenue of $500,000 or more
- Groups of CEOs of companies with annual sales revenue of $10+ million
- Groups of key executives—the C-suite
- Emerging leaders—next-generation leaders in first leadership role
- Small business owners of companies in the $1 to $10 million range
- Inside groups—Vistage groups within a large organization

In NYC one kind of Vistage group is a Trusted Advisor program that works with individual professionals, and "is designed to be a valuable resource for Vistage CEOs and business owners in NYC."

Mark Taylor, master chair of Vistage CEO groups in Manhattan, NYC, explained the requirements for those interested in participating in a professional service advisors' group. He said,

> It is not for everybody. Candidates are only invited to join after a selection process which includes an interview, attendance at a group meeting, and a reference check. In order to become a Vistage Trusted Advisor, individuals need to have a strong reputation in providing exceptional service, meeting and exceeding expectations and commitments and going beyond the call of duty. Another key aspect of these individuals is that they possess a strong CEO clientele in Manhattan and CEOs are their primary business focus.

The professional service providers program costs approximately $400/month, but if a member refers a CEO who joins Vistage the dues are waived for six months. In professional service providers groups, lawyers, accountants, and consultants follow the same peer advisor, facilitator-guided program as in the business executive groups. Members meet on a regular schedule, typically for a full or half day meeting, to network and learn new ways to approach common problems or opportunities.

> Your mastermind group is like having an objective board of directors, a success team, and a peer advisory group, all rolled into one.

22. Vistage website, https://www.vistage.com/.

Mark Taylor explained the process as follows. "Through a mastermind group process, first you create a goal, then a plan to achieve it. The group helps you with creative ideas and wise decision-making. Then, as you begin to implement your plan, you bring both success stories and problems to the group. Success stories are applauded 'loudly,' and problems are solved through peer brainstorming and collective, creative thinking."

In addition to interacting at meetings, members are expected to meet one-on-one in-between. Vistage is not a class or a "leads wanted" networking group. Usually leads and resources and joint projects develop but as a side benefit, not the main purpose.

Vistage membership is relatively expensive in terms of time and money commitments, but their website says the rewards are real. They claim that "Vistage member companies grow 2.2x faster than average small and midsize businesses."[23]

Collaberex

Peer-to-peer groups are less expensive and less structured versions of mastermind groups. They explicitly combine peer group advice and support with business development objectives. One such group is Collaberex started in 2016 by Jonathan Rosen, a former Vistage Group chair. The mission of the group is to "bring people together to achieve their goals through collaboration because we believe collaboration with the ideal group of people will assure all group members succeed."[24]

The group has five guiding principles:

- Collaborative culture: The primary goal of the group is for everyone to achieve their individual goals through the support of the group as a whole.
- Accountability: Group members hold each other accountable to execute the action steps they promise to make to achieve their goals.
- Learning: Each member contributes their own insights and experience to group discussions, providing constructive suggestions for resolving individual business challenges.
- Relationships: Meaningful peer advisory discussion is the direct road map to meaningful relationships, which lead to high quality referrals.
- Confidentiality, honesty, trust.[25]

The peer-to-peer learning component is a looser version of mastermind groups, with a focus on lead generation that is closer to general networking

23. Vistage website home page, https://www.vistage.com.
24. From Collaberex materials email, December 24, 2017.
25. Ibid.

groups. "Only network with those who will know the decision makers YOU need to meet to increase your client base because all group members call on the same client targets."[26]

Collaborex members belong to specific groups but can also participate in entity-wide social hours. Jonathan, as the owner-facilitator, crafts the meeting agenda and runs the meetings, which are similar in structure to Vistage's.

> Peer advice will improve your business development strategies and get you introduced to the decision makers you want to meet.

Reasons to Join Mastermind Groups

Amy B. Goldsmith, IP lawyer at Tartar Krinsky & Drogin, says she finds Vistage to be her "most successful" networking group. She likes the structure, finding that the nature of the discussion and length of the meetings fosters trust and intimacy. Relationships grow "organically."

These groups are good vehicles for people who are comfortable sharing personal information about themselves with a group and who will welcome the wisdom of the group. Some of those interviewed had been in Vistage groups and left because they found the time commitment to be too much for them.

Chapter Summary

In this chapter we have looked at a variety of open membership networking groups, meaning that once you find one that seems to fit, you can join unless there is a one person per job category and "your spot" is filled.

People join these groups for three primary business-related reasons:

- To meet people who can help you grow your business
- To find resources for your business, your clients, or your personal life
- To form strong relationships with people who can provide referrals for you

Group styles vary widely from the highly structured, leads-focused BNI to the friendly, loosely organized WBN. All open membership groups have an information-sharing or learning component as part of their meeting agenda. Mastermind-style groups are built around the learning component. Led by a facilitator they spotlight one or two problems that are then discussed, analyzed, and resolved by the group.

---

26. https://collaberex.com/services/more-than-networking/.

In Chapter 6 we look at three kinds of groups where membership is usually by invitation: personal private groups; honorary societies; and social, philanthropic, cultural, religious, and civic nonprofit groups. In these groups there may be less personal participation, but they are useful in terms of strategic marketing for their value as reputation builders in the public marketplace.

In-Person Groups Continued

6

In this chapter we look at three in-person group categories: personal private groups, honorary societies, and nonprofits be they social, philanthropic, cultural, religious, or civic. Unlike the groups in Chapter 5, members are invited to join these groups. While many of them do not have an explicitly business networking orientation, strategic networking can occur. It depends on what you are looking for.

Small, Strong Links: Personal Groups Set Up by One Individual

Private networking groups are usually formed by a single individual to meet that person's needs at the time. The ABA Women Rainmakers' Committee, which created a program around this concept, defines this kind of group as:

> [A] group of people who serve as a sounding board for each other. They provide guidance and coaching to help each other identify goals, opportunities and actions to advance careers and attain life goals. They provide emotional support and accountability to each other. They may also share their network of contacts . . . , thereby expanding the networks and opportunities for everyone else.[1]

Through ongoing interaction, the members—usually a small group, most of whom knew each other before they formed as a group—create very strong, trust-based relationships with each other that lead to shared resources, clients,

1. "Memo" ABA, Women Rainmakers, Personal Board of Directors Program Initiative Committee, 2016.

leads, and work. The program format in their meetings is similar to peer advisory groups where members:

- Make introductions
- Identify personal or work goals
- Prioritize topics for a group discussion around the goals expressed
- Agree on ways to stay in touch between meetings.

In general groups, a member will have weak and strong ties to others. In a personal private group all the ties are strong because the group develops in a natural, authentic way. It tends to become the members' growth engine in terms of referrals and resources. Because the group's members are so closely intertwined it is imperative for the founder to select members that can and will help each other to be successful.

Several people I interviewed have created personal groups. For example, Larry Hutcher, a co-managing partner, has formed two personal leadership groups. The first one only has business owners, many of whom are clients of his. It is focused on learning to be better leaders. The 19 members meet twice a month. A trained psychiatrist sets the agenda and leads the meetings' group discussions.

Hutcher's second group is an off-shoot of the first one. It has similar members but is focused solely on networking for business—leads wanted and referrals. There are about 30 members, many of whom are the head of company sales departments. The program is similar to other groups: introductions, leads wanted, success stories, and then a topic for general discussion. This group meets for breakfast twice a month, because Larry considers the frequency necessary to sustain and grow their trusted advisor relationships.

Roger E. Barton, managing partner of Barton LLP, prefers to network with potential clients of his firm's services rather than with referral sources. To further this goal, he created the Leaders in Law Institute [LILI], which conducts forums on topics related to innovation in the business of law for in-house counsel. According to the group's website, "Its mission is to provide in-house legal teams with a resource to enable them to deliver greater value to their corporate clients. . . . The LILI initiative brings together Directors and Preferred Suppliers to reach the goal of corporate compliance and litigation efficiency."[2]

Ronald K. Stair, principal of Creative Plan Design Ltd, hosts another variety of personal group: the invitation luncheon group. His Thursday lunches at a Long Island, New York, restaurant bring together six to ten guests, each representing a different business or profession. His criteria for inviting people is that they be "referable," which to him means that they know how to make connections and introductions. They know how to listen for the unspoken emotional

2. From the website, https://www.leadersinlawinstitute.com/.

needs and help those people step around them to move forward. They have something unusual to sell or they themselves are people of value.

> The variety illustrated by these examples demonstrates the idiosyncratic nature of personal networking groups, each one customized to meet the needs and goals of the founding member. Because they require the founder to not only be sure of his or her needs but also to have a solid network to choose from, these groups are typically formed by rainmaker networkers.

Reasons to Join Personal Groups

Sophisticated networkers who have spent time in networking groups get to a point where they want to collaborate most often with those people they value the most. These groups can be the most effective of all because they are a product of already formed, close relationships rather than a place for developing relationships. Mutual respect, esteem, and networking know-how form the basis for the effectiveness of the group.

People who want to establish such a group should build it around the common goals and interests of those they want in the group. At the same time, they need to balance the strength of a personal networking group with weak links in other areas so that they don't close themselves off from opportunities for new thoughts and ideas.

Honorary Groups

Typically, honorary designations for lawyers, such as Linda Klein's memberships as a Fellow of the American Bar Foundation on the Board of Trustees of the College of Law Practice Management[3] add another credential to one's bio. Members of invitation-only groups are seen to have achieved a certain level of expertise and experience. This kind of visibility facilitates strategic networking plans that involve targeting people you don't know well. Such groups also provide events—conferences and continuing education classes—that facilitate introductions to people.

At the other end of the prestige scale are "honorary" societies that a person pays to join. The person receives a letter complimenting them for being admitted to the "honorary" society. The honor is free but to let people know you have received it and to be included on the group's published list you have to purchase

3. From her bio, https://www.bakerdonelson.com/Linda-A-Klein.

a plaque or some other physical indication of the award. The groups sometimes, but rarely, offer in-person meeting opportunities.

To outsiders these honors may seem equal in value to the invitation-only group memberships. However, those in your profession whom you might want as referrers usually know the difference between honorary society and pay to play plaques.

Reasons to Join Honorary Groups

Invitation-only groups primarily add luster and visibility. They tell the world that you are acknowledged by your peers as an outstanding practitioner in specific areas. Most honor societies hold at least one meeting a year at which members can network, enabling them to meet peers and people in their aspirational networks.

Social, Philanthropic, Cultural, Religious, and Civic Nonprofits

Most people active in work-related networking groups are also active in groups connected to their personal interests. These interactions often don't lead explicitly to business, but they do provide satisfaction, new friends and colleagues in their personal life sphere, and visibility in their communities—useful assets in the context of strategic networking. Most of the networkers interviewed for this book belong to at least one such organization.

Andrew C. Peskoe, a corporate lawyer, says that he has not chosen his nonprofit boards to find clients, and not surprisingly, his board service has not been a direct sources of business. Board membership provides a venue that showcases him as a business-oriented lawyer and educates him in new areas. He feels the time he gives is well spent because he comes away feeling he has both provided value and become more knowledgeable.

Stephen M. Smith, an accountant who serves on several arts-related boards, recommends the experience both for the chance to expand your store of knowledge and, over time as relationships mature, to obtain business.

Armanda C. Squadrilli, a real estate broker, only networks through special interest, niche groups built around shared values and pastimes. These include the Simons Motorcycle Club, CBST synagogue, and a local cattle dog owners group. These groups not only provide productive ground for close personal contacts built around shared experiences, but they also reinforce her brand: "I am different and fun."

Bonnie Hagen, COO of Bright Energy Services, is an active member of the UJA-Federation's Westchester Business and Professional Division. Bonnie says it is her favorite membership because "it helps everybody—everywhere—and it is fertile ground for business networking. It 'kills two birds with one stone.'"

Reasons to Join Social, Philanthropic, Cultural, Religious, and Civic Nonprofits

Through referrals, board members can help people to enhance the quality of their lives and also help them with work-related issues. Joining nonprofits is also a way of adding to work-life balance by having an organization-based obligation to spend time contributing to an idea or activity that is personally important. These organizations also offer opportunities to create close friendships with like-minded people. Some become personal friends; others become part of a person's work world as well.

If you are interested in joining a nonprofit board or committee, begin by looking through your network for people you know who have expressed an interest in the subject matter or have been on such boards. Look for someone to introduce you to people currently active in the organization. You may have to volunteer time and resources at a committee or project level before you become eligible for a leadership position.

Most of the interviewees belong to a variety of groups, which, like a patchwork quilt, include different types of members and advance different goals. Many are on nonprofit groups' boards that offer information and resources relevant to their workplace goals.[4]

Andrew C. Peskoe, a corporate lawyer with a large mergers and acquisitions practice and a core of technology and hospitality industry clients, sits on boards that relate to his professional expertise or relate to the technology or hospitality industry. Through these groups he hears about activities and individuals important to his work.

Bonnie Hagen, COO of Bright Energy Services, belongs to industry and trade association groups where her clients and colleagues are. She has also been appointed to local government committees and boards that impact her company's services. In addition, she belongs to general mixed membership networking groups. Her mix of organizations enables her to balance her core relationships

4. Information taken from their LinkedIn profiles, firm websites, and personal interviews with the author.

with a wide array of weak links, ensuring that she stays abreast of the fast-changing technology in her field.

Chapter Summary

In Chapters 4, 5, and 6, we discussed various kinds of in-person organizations and reasons why you might select one kind rather than another. We also discussed the advantages of active, thoughtful participation in whatever groups you join and looked at the average group participation cycle. In the next chapter, we explore online group activities and how to meld in-person and online networking groups.

Online Networking Venues

7

In the 21st century, online networking has emerged as a substitute for or complement to in-person networking. For many individuals who grew up with the Internet and smartphones, connecting via social media is as natural as breathing. For some of them, in-person networking seems artificial and uncomfortable. Vik Rajan, a co-founder of PhoneBlogger.net, explained that "millennials don't see the need for formal in-person networking since they are always connected on the Internet, and they see these relationships as real relationships." As David Abeshouse, a mediator and arbitrator, says about the younger generation: "They think in-person networking is passé, but they will see it differently once they try in-person meetings."

For the parents of those individuals, the Internet is more likely to be an acquired taste, understood to be a networking tool, but less effective in their minds than in-person networking. These are the people who find humor in the classic New Yorker cartoon with two dogs in front of the computer screen. One dog, with his paw on the keyboard, says to the other, "On the Internet nobody knows you're a dog."[1]

Regardless of age, most networkers share the perception that you need to pay attention to social media in order to learn what is going on, to keep abreast of trends, and to research people and businesses you network with online or off-line. In this chapter, we review online networking opportunities and consider some of the ways to link online and off-line networking for maximum effectiveness.

1. Peter Steiner cartoon, *The New Yorker*, July 5, 1993.

Social Media Today

According to eMarketer, US Social Usage StatPack,[2] by 2020 over 200 million people will be social network users. Increasing usage is tied to smartphones. The StatPack data show that "in 2016, 87.1% of social network users accessed social sites via mobile phone."[3]

There are many definitions of social media. We are using the StatPack definitions. They define *social* networks as "sites where the primary activities involve creating a profile and interacting with a network of contacts by sharing status updates, comments, photos or other content."[4] Social network users are defined as "Internet users of any age who use social networks via any device at least once a month."[5]

Many people use social media just for personal conversations, but the web is also an excellent venue for business and professional purposes, including the following:

- To leverage the national and international breadth of the web to compete outside your local area
- To build an online audience interested in your thought leadership, your products, or your online relationships with others
- To position yourself as an expert
- To make career moves and follow the careers of colleagues and friends
- To connect or reconnect with people from all three network sources: the personal, the occupational, and the aspirational
- To research and keep up with ideas, places, people
- To establish an expanded personal presence
- To keep in touch through relevant content posted to your contacts and through invitations to events
- To stay visible and top of mind

The professionals I interviewed ran the gamut of social media use, from those who don't use social media at all to those who prefer it to in-person networking. Those who prefer online networking cite the time saved because they don't have to travel to and from a meeting place. And, they can connect from anywhere—in their car, on a train, walking down the street. They also appreciate the breadth of contacts and visibility options that are available online.

2. Data from eMarketer US Social Usage StatPack, 2017, eMarketer Inc., https://www.emarketer.com/Report/US-Social-StatPack-Usage-Ad-Spending-2016-2020/2001999.

3. Ibid.

4. Ibid.

5. Ibid.

David Rosenbaum pointed out that "social media has changed the world of networking. Younger people communicate via social media, preferring texting to talk, and accept the social profiles they see online.

David Abeshouse, a mediator, is representative of those who see social media networking as an activity that "giveth and taketh away." The possibilities for misinformation are "bad," while the ability to broaden your intellectual and geographic reach is "good."

Those who use social media sparingly or not at all cite peoples' ability to create false images of themselves and share false data so you can't be sure who you are really talking to. They also find in-person meetings more productive. In fact, "around nine in ten people say small meetings are their favorite communication method."[6]

Richard Friedman, an employment law litigator, uses social media to share promotional material and event announcements and to research individuals and law firms before he meets someone for coffee. He doesn't use LinkedIn or other sites as sources of introductions. He prefers to meet people in person because in person he "can see how a person seems. Is the person a smart, sophisticated lawyer or businessperson? Are they likely to know other lawyers? Are they open to giving and getting introductions?"

Online Options and Activities

Internet networking sites run the gamut from open social networks to private groups that communicate online. Open networks include the obvious—LinkedIn and Facebook—as well as industry or activity specific directories such as AVVO and LegalZoom for lawyers, platforms for disseminating content such as Justia and LexBlog, and listservs that share knowledge informally among members of a group.

There are also private groups that meet online. For example, a dozen lawyers who met each other on Solosez now prefer to meet privately as an online mastermind-style group. Another example is LawyerSmack, "a private community for attorneys interested in discussing practice-related issues with their peers

6. Aja Frost, "15 Surprising Stats on Networking and Face-To-Face Communications," https://blog.hubspot.com/sales/face-to-face-networking-stats.

in real time."[7] The home page identifies four advantages of their private group discussions:

- Inspiration: Camaraderie and mentorship with hundreds of lawyers.
- Learning: Brainstorm problems and discover solutions with lawyers across practice areas and around the world.
- Privacy: Engage in safe and secure discussions among peers.
- A Thriving Discussion Forum: There are 100+ channels dedicated to legal topics. . . . There are also channels dedicated to non-legal topics such as fashion, gaming, pop culture and more. Users exchange over 15,000 messages weekly.[8]

Another example of an online networking community is VNO—Virtual Networking Organization—offering the online equivalent of peer-to-peer in-person groups. Its website offers the following summary of benefits:

VNO TEAMS—YOUR "PERSONAL BOARD OF DIRECTORS"

Your VNO Team Provides:

- Category Exclusivity in Your Professional Niche
- Weekly Video Meeting Focused on Relationship Building and Referrals
- Fun and Effective Team Building Exercises
- 24/7 Access to a Private Discussion Forum Exclusively for Your VNO Team
- The Opportunity to Lead Your Own VNO Team in 3–6 Months—Doubling Your Referral Opportunities
- An All-Purpose Support Network—Your "Personal Board of Directors"
- Join Us Today for Just a Few Dollars Per Week—"Coffee & Doughnut" Money[9]

These are only two of millions of online networking sites.[10] There are many available lists of other useful, well-regarded online networking sites. For example, one list for entrepreneurs offers a wide-ranging variety of sites:

---

7. Ari Kaplan, "LawyerSmack Is Reinventing the Way Lawyers Communicate," March 16, 2018, http://www.abajournal.com/news/article/reinventing_the_way_lawyers_communicate/.
8. LawyerSmack home page, https://www.lawyersmack.com/.
9. "VNO Teams," https://vno.wildapricot.org/directory.
10. Google Searches: "online business networking sites" = 5.9 million results, "online networking groups" = 3.4 million results.

- Quora—"Quora's mission is to share and grow the world's knowledge."[11] You can follow whatever interests you and then engage with people who follow you.
- Plaxo is an online address book with room to add contacts' birthdays.
- Viadeo—A French language site, similar to LinkedIn, used by French professionals.
- XING—Calls itself the "platform for business networking," used by professionals in Germany, Austria, and Switzerland.[12]
- EFactor—an "entrepreneur-focused social network to connect, educate, service and help fund entrepreneurs."[13]
- LocalsNetworking—members build their own referral network in their communities.

Most in-person networking groups have websites where the public can learn about the group and members can connect online. Many also offer member-only listservs. For example, both Gotham City Networking, Inc., and Westchester Business Network have listservs where their members post announcements, requests, and thank-you messages.

Some groups that meet in person use social media sites such as Meetup.com to attract members, announce their schedules, and register for specific activities. For example, Dan Lear, Avvo Director of Industry Relations, uses Meetup to find and connect with a combination of lawyers and tech people in his hometown of Seattle who focus on innovation.

Most people considering online networking activities turn first to Facebook or LinkedIn, so we will look at the business networking opportunities they present.

Facebook

Facebook offers opportunities to join social, community, and demographic-focused groups, such as Mom meetups or skateboarders or eldercare caretakers, that introduce you to a community where people with similar interests converse. The group gets to know you as a member of their shared-interest, so when you answer a question related to your work expertise, your reply is believable because it assumes the mantle of the group's trust-based discussions. Many professionals who have individuals as clients also join such groups to gain a feel for what their clients are thinking and how they are talking about subjects important to them.

11. https://www.quora.com/What-is-the-main-purpose-of-Quora.

12. Christine Hueber, "Which of the Top 5 Professional Networking Sites – LinkedIn, Quora, Plaxo, Viadeo, XING – is best for your business?," https://www.christinehueber.com/which-of-the-top-5-professional-networking-sites-linkedin-quora-plaxo-viadeo-xing-is-best-for-your-business-by-christine-hueber/, October 11, 2013; see also, Albert Costill, "12 Professional Networking Alternatives to LinkedIn," https://www.searchenginejournal.com/12-professional-networking-alternatives-linkedin/139681/, September 15, 2015.

13. http://www.marketwired.com/press-release/efactor-groups-social-networks-division-surpasses-20-million-members-otcqb-efct-2066181.htm.

Most people think of Facebook as just a forum for individual communications, but it also offers the option to create professional or corporate profiles under your company name. Company pages offer links to About, Photos, Follow Us, Company News, Posts, YouTube, and Community, where visitors can learn more about a company, its personnel, and its culture.

Stacey Cohen, a public relations expert, has a personal page and a company page. The company page includes interesting news articles as well as updates related to her company.

Stacy Francis, a financial planner, also has two Facebook pages with similar information. Both feature many videos as well as opportunities to "like" or sign up for activities mentioned on the business site.

It's easy to set up your own Facebook group.[14] Most of the lawyers interviewed have a personal Facebook page and most of the firms have a company Facebook page. You can create a standalone group or one within your corporate page. Here's how:

- Create a description for the group and a set of rules and expectations.
- Define who you want to attract, going back to your goals and your target persona to make sure your definition is as specific as possible. For example, "All unhappy married women who live on Long Island" is too vague. Better: "Long Island women thinking about divorce."
- Use content to draw members. Post regularly and encourage members to comment and post.
- Verify potential members to make sure they are not fake profiles or spammers.
- Connect with each new member to set expectations.

In addition, most online groups have Facebook links. For example, Lawyerist, a networking site for small-firm lawyers, sent out a recruiting email that asked: "So, if you want to talk with similarly different-minded lawyers about your law practice, please join us. If you haven't already, just sign up to become a Lawyerist Insider (it's free!), *then join our private Facebook group* for solo and small firm lawyers in the US and Canada. We can't wait to meet you."[15]

---

14. References material from www.becomeablogger.com, "How to Use Facebook Groups to Build Your Audience [infographic]," reprinted on https://www.socialmediatoday.com/news/how-to-use-facebook-groups-to-build-your-audience-infographic/520015/. See also, Sarah Dawley, "Using Micro-communities to Boost Organic Reach on Social Media," https://blog.hootsuite.com/micro-communities-organic-reach-social/.

15. Email sent May 18, 2018.

LinkedIn

LinkedIn is the largest professional networking online site, with more than 400 million members. All but two of the three dozen people I interviewed are on LinkedIn. They use the site to:

- Connect to people they know or want to meet
- Circulate articles and event invitations
- Circulate updates about what's happening in their work world
- Follow the news
- Research people, companies, and places as part of their in-person networking preparations
- Begin a dialogue with thought leaders
- Make referrals and get referred
- Join and participate in groups that are important to them or to their niche markets

James K. Landau, a litigator, explains how he grew his contact list by using the opportunities presented by LinkedIn. As diagramed in Figure 7.1, Jim would peruse the contacts of people he linked with to identify people he would like to meet. He would then contact the person who owned that list and suggest that he or she look at Jim's list and make a similar selection. The next step was to schedule a breakfast or lunch at which the two people who knew each other would invite two of their contacts that their colleague wanted to meet. At the breakfast six people would have a chance to get to know each other. Jim thinks the ability to share contact lists "speeds up the relationship process and provides a means to build a contact list quickly. But it is time consuming—and you still need to develop the relationship."

Figure 7.1 Sharing Contacts on LinkedIn

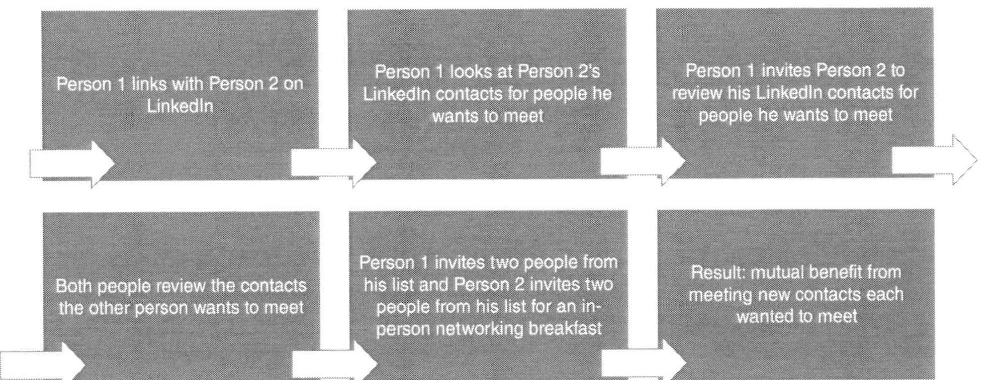

Several of the interviewees use LinkedIn in creative ways.

Stacey Cohen has over 20,000 LinkedIn contacts. She uses her list for three purposes:

- To grow her brand by recycling her publications and sharing her *HuffPost* articles
- To share knowledge in LinkedIn groups by answering questions and linking people with similar interests
- To identify individuals she wants to interview for her *HuffPost* article.

To enhance her own activity, she uses paid campaigns to acquire followers on Twitter and Facebook.

Marcia R. Golden stressed her use of LinkedIn to build relationships. She doesn't want to link to people she doesn't know at all. So, when she gets a LinkedIn invitation to connect from someone she doesn't know she responds by calling the person or sending them a reply message suggesting they talk on the phone or meet for coffee first.

Abby Rosmarin similarly connects to people she knows because it is socially expected. "I stopped participating in LinkedIn except when someone requests a connection and there is a precise and meaningful communication about the desire to connect."

Stacy Francis sees online networking as a very important way to stay in touch. She "goes where her clients go" and uses content to reach out to clients and referral sources to keep abreast of what others in her network are doing. Stacy's formula for online content is 15 percent promotional and 85 percent sharing resources, inspirational quotes, and articles that serve to nurture her relationships.

There are literally thousands of LinkedIn groups. LinkedIn allows you to join up to 50 groups. Of course, join your alumni groups, professional associations and online groups that parallel in-person groups and organizations you belong to. Then, look for groups with like-minded people in similar professions. Through these groups you may meet potential referral sources or resources for you and your client.

It is unlikely that you will participate in all of them. For example, Marc Halpert belongs to 50 groups, but he is only active in 10 to 15 of them. You, too, should choose a few to be active in. For those few, take 15 minutes a day to follow discussions and contribute when appropriate. Post content yourself to share useful information, but also to demonstrate your willingness to be part of the group. Contribute often enough and your participation will be highlighted on your group's discussion page.

Particularly if you have a B2C focus, you may want to seek out groups built around the interests of those you want to work with and for. Participating in these conversations will provide an opportunity to know your target audience better in terms of their interests, their opinions, their "hotspots," and their use of language when talking with each other. This kind of learning helps you blend into your prospects' and clients' worlds.

Join personal interest groups that focus on sailing or chess or parenting or social issues where you can share common interests. People in these groups may become friends and, in some cases, clients or referral sources as well.

LinkedIn groups are also excellent sources of information and innovative ideas. Join the groups that people you follow for their ideas belong to. When you identify other interesting people in the group conversations, link to them and, if possible, invite them to join you for an in-person coffee.

Online Research

LinkedIn and other networking sites offer excellent options for researching people before you meet them. Use the opportunity to learn about breakfast and lunch colleagues, guest speakers, members of networking groups you visit, group leaders, and so on.

- Read their online bios for a sense of what is important to them.
- Scroll down to the personal section to learn something about their private life.
- If, as on LinkedIn, a site shows you share contacts, be sure to make a note about this so you can begin a conversation on common ground.
- If you have never met in person, pay attention to the person's photograph so you will recognize them when you meet.

Online the equivalent of assessing a person in the flesh is reading other people's opinions of them in testimonials or recommendations. We all remember stories of people who have been duped into believing that the pedophile online was a nice friendly young man. The antidote to this kind of deception is to know the person through the comments about them.

As Vik Rajan says, "Trust the aggregate." Add to these opinions people's likes and shares and comments on posts and you can begin to get a sense of the person.

Use Google search to find articles by and about your contacts. Be sure to check some of the pages behind page 1 where you will probably find interesting information about their "previous lives." For example, I googled myself on May 18, 2018, and the search registered 99,300 results. Of course, there are erroneous entries and duplicates, but, even so, if you look at later pages you can find links to my postdoctoral research, previous jobs, and volunteer pursuits. The point is that more in-depth perusing in Google searches can unearth capabilities you didn't know the contact had and perhaps lead to new shared interests.

Online Networking Etiquette

Just as in-person networking assumes a certain attitude and etiquette, so too, does online networking. Personalization is important in both settings. For example, when you invite someone to link to you, it is a best practice to add a few words about where you have met or who you know in common or why you want to connect with them.

When someone has looked at your LinkedIn profile, consider sending them a message saying, "Thank you for taking the time to review my profile. Can I help you in any way?" (or) "Would you like to meet for coffee?" If someone adds an online testimonial for you, send a message thanking them for their help.

When you participate in online conversations, use them as an opportunity to showcase your expertise or personal experience with the issue at hand. Don't say "Great article." Instead say, "Great article because [and then give a reason]." Your reasoning becomes a billboard showing everyone else in the group how you think and how you feel about issues relevant enough to be shared in the group. A thoughtful conversation thread becomes a reputation builder establishing you as an expert.

Blending Online and In-Person Activities

"No matter how advanced our methods of communication have become, nothing seems to have come close to replicating the value of face-to-face contact."[16] Researchers generally agree that there is a psychological difference between online and in-person relationships. Social media facilitates connections but creates little emotional involvement.[17] By contrast, in-person encounters provide physiological benefits.

16. http://www.virgin.com/entrepreneur/infographic-importance-face-face-networking.

17. See Nick Morgan, "What's Wrong with Virtual Communication, Parts 1 and 2," http://www.publicwords.com/2018/04/10/whats-wrong-with-virtual-communication-part-1/ and http://www.publicwords.com/2018/04/12/whats-wrong-with-virtual-communication-part-2/.

Your blood pressure goes down, you have synchrony, you mimic your friend's posture unconsciously. It's a rapport humans have developed over thousands of years, and you don't get that when you only follow someone on social media."[18]

To network most effectively, online and in-person activities should complement and reinforce each other. Ivan Misner, the founder of BNI, thinks that online and face-to-face marketing are "a 'both/and.'"[19] He thinks a new kind of group will evolve online. He calls them "walled-gardens" because they will be "mini-social sites that are niche-oriented. . . . The attraction to groups like this will be the niche orientation and the shared values and/or the mission of the organizations. "The technology will allow greater connections—while the face-to-face will allow deeper connections."[20]

Many online organizations hold in-person events, and many in-person organizations use online options to form groups, send invitations, and so on. For example, Network After Work, a national organization with over four million members in over 100 U.S. cities, organized an event in Seattle called "Meet Your LinkedIn Connections."[21] A group called Deliberate Solos uses email to invite people to in-person events.[22]

The person you present online should be a replica of you at your best in person. The competencies you list online should be obvious when people talk to you in person about the benefits they can expect from your expertise.

When you meet in person, invite people to connect with you online. When you meet online and want to make sure there is a fit with your strategic networking, plan an in-person meeting or phone call.

LinkedIn makes it easy to casually keep in touch between in-person meetings. For example, you can:

- Use online personalization reminders to send birthday cards, anniversary cards, and other appropriate personal cards to people you know.
- When you learn through online sites that people change jobs or marry or have children, send a note or a personalized card.
- Send holiday cards, not just for Christmas, but for New Year's or Valentine's Day or the Fourth of July.

---

18. Carlin Flora quoted in Teddy Wayne, "Are My Friends Really My Friends?" *The New York Times*, May 13, 2018.

19. Ivan Misner, "Three Networking Trends to Watch," December 27, 210, https://www.entrepreneur.com/article/217783

20. Ibid.

21. Email from Network After Work—Seattle, April 16, 2018, https://www.networkafterwork.com.

22. Greenwald email from Deliberate Solos, May 14, 2018.

Just as in-person networking is built around the give-to-get principle, so, too, take advantage of Internet opportunities to share knowledge and make introductions. Use the reach of the Internet to extend the possibilities that turn up with in-person networking.

Think globally. Online offers a way to extend your reach beyond your local geographic area. Follow global trends online if it is appropriate for your business. When you travel, search your online contacts for people who live where you are going, and connect. Before conferences, research who else from your hometown will be there and plan to connect; or check if people on your own contact lists will be there. Then reach out to them to plan to meet in person at the event.

Combining the advantages of online and in-person networking makes each connection richer. Use the breadth of the Internet to build your weak links, and the depth of in-person connections to reinforce your networking core. See "Helpful Hints for Online Networking" in Appendix 3, pages 211–212.

Preparation for Strategic Conversations 8

Random networking can be frustrating—so much time, so many people, so few who matter. You can minimize the problem of getting lost among the vast number of networking choices. Focus your activities on the most perfect kind of client or referral source for you. Centering your networking efforts on specific companies, topics, people, or places concentrates your actions on what will be best for you. This is the essence of strategic networking.

In this chapter, to help you focus your networking we look at four key preparation questions:

- What are the characteristics of your target persona—a construct that represents a composite of the major characteristics of your target audience?
- What is your value proposition? What do you offer that people want?
- How do you capture your value proposition in a short "elevator pitch"?
- What stories can you tell to demonstrate your usefulness to your target persona clients?

Reviewing Your Goals and Plan

You should begin by revisiting Chapter 2, paying attention to three segments:

- Worksheet 2.5, your SWOT analysis, which lets you look at your personal strengths and weaknesses in the context of the opportunities and threats in the competitive arena
- Worksheet 2.2, Your Work—because you probably want to target either additional clients like your current favorites or referrers who can introduce you to such people
- Worksheet 2.7, your marketing action plan

Returning to these specifics gives context and specificity to your networking activities; and ensures that your activities are cumulative in impact.

In order to create useful networking tools, as discussed later in the chapter, you need to expand on your understanding of your current clients. You want to look more closely at the 20 percent of your client base that provides 80 percent of your revenue. Fill in Table 8.1 Sample 80/20 Clients [Appendix 2, page 194] to get a better perspective on the characteristics of your current client base.

Filled in, your table might look like this:

Table 8.1 Sample 80/20 Clients

Client name	Industry/ SIC or NAICS #*	Number of years as a client	Services used and services client could use	Factors influencing ability to get additional work
Charlie Brown Inc.	Comic books NAICS: 323111**	5	NOW: Contracts, intellectual property FUTURE: M&A	Introduction to M&A group. Expand contacts at company, continue to offer proactive advice
Samson Haircuts	Beauty salon NAICS: 812112	4	NOW: Contracts, loan documents FUTURE: employment law, financing alternatives	Introduce to employment practice lawyers, provide financing advice, introduce owner to bankers and accountants
Big Blue Natural Gas Company	Natural gas distribution NAICS: 221210	8	NOW: Regulatory services, agreements with other suppliers FUTURE: geographic expansion, M&A	Expand contacts at the company, introduce members of the team, research trends and relevant state and federal regulations, provide proactive advice

*SIC stands for Standard Industrial Classification, NAICS stands for the North American Industry Classification System "[which] is the standard used by Federal statistical agencies in classifying business establishments for the purpose of collecting, analyzing, and publishing statistical data related to the U.S. business economy." Home page at https://www.census.gov/eos/www/naics/.
**Found at https://www.naics.com/naics-search-results/.

Analyzing this data in conjunction with your SWOT analysis will suggest the type of client you want to duplicate, the service areas you may want to emphasize, and potential pitfalls and possibilities in pursuing more clients in this category. Keeping your goals and targets in mind, you can prepare some basic materials for use in connecting with these targets. Use this analysis to ground your planning.

In addition to your own thoughts about clients and referral sources you can, and should, do some research. Examine a variety of sources, including:

- Your website analytics to see where visitors come from and what they look at
- The social media habits of current clients and referral sources
- Where current clients go for believable information
- What kind of relationship current 80/20 clients want with you
- The nature of current 80/20 clients' interests and concerns
- Information in your contacts database about the clients you are using as a guide for your persona, such as how they came to be a client, how the relationship has grown, and what their concerns are
- Public information about the company, industry, or demographic you are profiling

Once you've reviewed your specific interests and done research as to the general framework in which you will be seeking business, you can create your first networking tool—a persona.

Target Personas

Strategic networking centers your efforts on connecting with people like your ideal clients or referral sources who can introduce you to the people you want to target. To make meaningful connections, you need to understand these people—who they are; where they live; what they like; who they believe; how they talk about problems and opportunities; and where they go for information, resources, and assistance.

One way to make this easier to figure out is to create a target persona that is a composite representation of your ideal client or referral source. Target personas make it simpler to draw connections between you and your targets because they help you identify both the emotional and rational aspects of your target audience. You use the process of creating personas to put yourself in the target's shoes. Understanding what is important to them helps you formulate solutions they will value.

Because the persona is a device to narrow your focus, you will probably want to create two personas—one for the ideal client and one for the ideal referrer. Each persona is a fictional composite of the characteristics of your networking target audience. Regardless of whether your target is a company or an individual, you want to create a realistic representation of the entity or person—warts and all. You should give each persona a gender and a name. Try to find a picture or photo that looks like your image of your persona.

A persona has both tangible and intangible attributes. In addition to the physical attributes you also need to understand how they think, what they like and dislike, how they shop for advisors, and where they go for fun and knowledge. These intangibles help you to understand what resonates with them—what bothers them, what they need, and how they go about addressing their needs.

Use the questions on Worksheet 8.1 Characteristics of Your Target Persona [Appendix 2, pages 195–196] as a guide for building your personas. Sidebar 8.1 is an example of a persona for a woman lawyer in a corporate job. You want to work with other companies like hers, and you usually interact with lawyers at her level, so you want a persona that resembles lawyers like her.

Sidebar 8.1 Sample Persona

What is her name? Lucy Smith

What does she look like? Let's say that she looks like Lucille Ball of *I Love Lucy* fame—curly red hair, blue eyes, attractive *[You might want to find a magazine photo that looks like your imaginary person.]*

How old? Early 30s

How educated? Law degree from NYU School of Law, Vassar College

Where does she work and live? She works in Manhattan, lives in Harrison, NY.

What are her living arrangements? She is married to a wealth advisor at Wells Fargo bank.

Who is in her family and what role do they play in her life? She is close to her parents and siblings and often uses them as sounding boards.

Who are the key influencers in the persona's life? Her older sister and her best friend, both business executives.

How do they influence her buying decisions? They are all making good salaries but feeling poor compared to friends who work at hedge funds. So, they go prowling for clothes and furniture in secondhand stores and open markets. Always looking for a bargain and driving hard bargains as they bid down the price of purchases.

What motivates this persona? A desire to succeed and also a desire to be liked and respected for her contributions.

What are her interests outside of work? Swimming, skiing, the Yankees.

What hobbies? She collects pitchers.

How do these interests impact how she interacts with the world around her? They effect how she spends her free time. She tries to swim once or twice a week after work. She knows all the Yankee batting stats going back 15 years. Her firm has Yankee series tickets, which she often uses as a way to spend networking time with clients.

How does she feel about major societal forces such as politics, religion, discrimination? She is a fiscal conservative but leans liberal on social issues.

What are her hot buttons? She doesn't like to be taken advantage of, or treated differently than her male co-workers.

What makes the persona happy? A job well-done, time with friends and family, vacations in interesting places.

Is she a penny pincher or a spendthrift? Thrifty.

How does she prefer to pay for purchases? Credit card with airline miles attached.

Where does she go for information related to purchases? Facebook, online newsletters, and her best friends.

What social media platforms does she participate on? LinkedIn, Facebook

Does she tend to be a lurker, commentator, or creator on social media? Lurker, unless she feels very strongly about the issue.

Who does she work for? Charlie Brown Inc.

Industry? Comic book publisher, NAICS 323111.

What does she do for a living? She is an inhouse corporate lawyer.

What is her title at work? Associate general counsel.

What does she do during an average workday? She works on corporate issues related to contracts and mergers and acquisitions.

What are his key responsibilities and challenges? She manages a group of four male junior attorneys who often challenge her authority.

What kind of rewards and frustrations are related to her work? She is overworked, underpaid, and frustrated by the lack of respect she feels she gets from her male peers. She gets great satisfaction from work well done. She is also an excellent mentor to junior executives and a confident leader.

Does she make or influence buying decisions? Indirectly, by contributing to the information upon which decisions are made. She has responsibility for many important initiatives, but her boss and the CEO are the final decision makers. Her input is well received and respected.

How important is her job to her identity? Relatively important.

How much money does she make? $175,000 annual salary + bonus.

What media does she go to for information? Online references, topical blogs and newsletters, print newspapers, American Bar Association materials.

What communication device(s) does she prefer to use? Her phone.

Does she read physical books or magazines or newspapers, or does she prefer digital media options? She enjoys physical books for pleasure, but does most of her work-related reading and research online.

How does she want to be contacted? By email to set up a time to talk.

What are her current needs? She is tasked with doing the research related to a decision to undertake a possible merger.

What can you do to meet those needs? We can share our insights regarding other similar mergers and prepare some of the background research for her. We can also draw up a first draft of the research memo.

How will you communicate to her your ability to help her? We will set up a phone meeting with her to discuss her role and explain how we can make her life easier.

Show your persona profile to other people in your firm to get their input. Have conversations with the current clients you are thinking about as you create your persona's goals, values, pain points, and lifestyle.

The devil is in the details. Each persona should be as carefully delineated as possible. Delving into even the smallest details will help you begin to believe in the reality of your persona. Details serve two functions:

- First, they help you begin to understand your target audience's motivations, issues, interests, and problems so that you have a better understanding of their thoughts, feelings, and behaviors.
- Second, creating a persona can help you find previously undetected tactical opportunities for your services that make them more useful and relevant to your target's life.

Your persona is ready when you can use it to answer a key question: "Where does your product or service constructively intersect with what Lucy does or what Lucy cares about?" The process of creating a persona helps you figure out the best places to find your targets and the most effective ways to communicate with them. You will begin to appreciate how they like to be spoken to, what they value, and how best to reach them. This knowledge becomes the basis for germane elevator pitches, stories, and marketing content that make it easier for you to create important relationships.

Understanding the persona's personality and issues can help you to determine how to move forward. Using our Lucy persona shows how you can answer key questions such as:

- What kind of research will you need to do to get a sense of the context in which her company operates?
  - We will review government data on the comic book and publishing industry, websites of her company and her company's competitors, deal lists, and similar information to get a sense of deal particulars in this industry, and Google her social media presence.
- What kinds of communication will you have with her?
  - We will send her useful stats on M&A in the comic book industry, and background sheets on some new regulations that may impact any merger.
- How will you secure in-person meetings?
  - She attends her industry trade association meetings. Our law firm is an associate member of the association. We plan to invite her to sit with us at the next meeting. We would also like to tell her of our shared passion for the Yankees and see if that leads to an invitation to join her in her firm's box seats.
- Who else do you need to meet?
  - We need to meet her merger team—the lawyers and the businesspeople. We also need to talk with her boss and his boss, the CEO. We want to introduce her to our M&A team and offer some suggestions to make the merger more cost effective. We want to be sure to include women on our team.

Your Value Proposition

A value proposition is the connector between what you do and its impact on what your clients think and do. It is the glue in any professional relationship because it relates your expertise to your clients' expectations regarding the benefits they will derive from that expertise. As J.P. Morgan, the American banker, said: "I don't know as I want a lawyer to tell me what I cannot do. I hire him to tell me how to do what I want to do."

Everyone defines value differently because the definition is subjective. One person's idea of expensive is another person's idea of reasonable. Value is a person's idiosyncratic perception of the worth of a service in relation to its cost—cost in terms of time, money, effort, and result. Value is assessed by clients based on their expectations coming into the relationship balanced by their view of their shared experience with you and your firm.

As an equation it can be expressed as: performance plus results divided by client's expectations equals the client's perception of the value of a service.

$$\frac{\text{Performance} + \text{Results}}{\text{Client's Expectations}} = \text{Client's Perception of Value}$$

Value takes many forms. For some people your professional advice is more important than the actual final result. For others, the end result is most important. Some people assess your client service manner and attention and assume that courtesy, empathy, and intelligent questioning indicate strong professional bona fides.

> Marc W. Halpert, LinkedIn trainer, says, 'Offer people something they need even if they don't know they want it. Be understood and credible so that what you say sticks in their mind.'

Typically, when a professional is asked what they do for a living they respond to the "do" verb. They say, "I am a lawyer or a litigator or an accountant or a financial planner." While this is true, it is not really an answer to the question behind the question which is: "Why do I care about what you do? Will what you do help me in any way?" The answer they can relate to is about the *why* of what you do—what motivates and excites you about your work—and the *what for*—the benefits that result from what you do.

Because these sub rosa questions are more emotionally compelling to the client, your value proposition should focus on the *why* and the *what for*. A strong value proposition may include any or all of the following content:

- Why you do what you do—your motivations
- What you do and how you approach what you do
- Discussion of the problem itself and its impact
- Results—tangible and intangible that the client can anticipate from your work
- Stories of similar work with other clients
- Numbers or percentages to demonstrate your successes in solving x problem or addressing y issue.

In formulating your initial value proposition, begin with what your persona wants—what is s/he looking for and what will s/he value. Use Worksheet 8.2

Features/Benefits Comparison [Appendix 2, page 197] to move from what you do to how it will benefit the client and how your resolution of the issues will satisfy your client's rational and emotional requirements.

Note that in filling out the worksheet, for each "what you do" entry there may be multiple benefits, some of which resolve the same client issues and some of which will be irrelevant to her. Record them all. Some results will answer the target's values perfectly, others will not. Be sure to note instances where a mismatch occurs between what you can offer and what she wants or needs. You will want to return to this analysis often, and update it as you prepare for specific networking activities and meetings with specific individuals.

Table 8.2 is an example of how you might fill out a features/benefits comparison table.

Table 8.2 Features/Benefits Comparison

Your attributes	Features of your practice	Benefits of these activities for the target	Relationship to the target's wants, needs, and desires
What you do	Mergers and acquisitions corporate work	Your expertise Results for clients	Reasons the target gives for wanting your assistance
Why you do it	Get satisfaction from being part of business' growth plans	Your previous experience and research expertise	She wants her research to be valued and used to make the decision as to a merger or not
What you know	Experience with successfully handling similar matters Expertise Knowledge of the client's interests in securing certain results History of working with her	Experience working with her on previous matters Perceptive about and understanding of her work-related needs and her underlying worries about the importance of her role in the merger process	Your understanding of her triggers Your answer to her WIIFM—What's in it for me?
Your approach to client service	Your responsiveness and willingness to go the extra mile	The "extras" you provide so your clients feel well served and valued	How you demonstrate your value to the client

The process of creating a chart such as this helps you to bring the general features of your daily practice down to this specific application of your skill set and experience. As you fill in the chart, be conscious of both the business rationality and personal emotions of your target. To be successful you will need to meet the business needs of this matter by showing empathy for her personal situation.

Elevator Speech

The concept envisions you in an elevator traveling to the 20th floor explaining your work to someone else in the same elevator in a way that piques the other person's interest. The moving elevator visual alludes to speed. The close intimate setting of an elevator suggests forced spatial intimacy and a need to be succinct and relevant to the other person.

What's in It for Me? [WIIFM]: When you are trying to interest someone else in your work, it is important to remember always that other people care less about what you do and more about how what you do impacts them. A common marketing axiom assumes that people are concerned with their own world 80 percent of the time. We call this perspective a person's WIIFM. Everyone has one. Your personas will help you understand your target's WIIFM.

You want to do a 180 degree mind flip and think about your service or product from the customer's point of view. Why would they want it? How will they use it? Do they need it?

Walking through Edinburgh airport many years ago, I saw a wonderful IBM ad that speaks directly to WIIFM: It said:

STOP selling what you have.

START selling what they need.

Knowing how your personas think and feel provides a baseline for crafting a meaningful message for your target market. An elevator speech should be an answer to your target's WIIFM.

An elevator speech has three aspects to it:

- It's a sound bite or slogan that encapsulates both your *why* and *what for*. It needs to be authentic. Hopefully it is catchy enough that people will remember it. "Just do it," or "A diamond is forever," or "We try harder." All these are examples of a product pitched from the customer's point of view.
- It should invite a question, such as: "Why did you decide to litigate on behalf of orphan children?" or "Why does it matter if my employment contract doesn't include reasons for my termination?"

- It's short: think 30 seconds, 150–250 words—more like a television commercial than a press release. Remember that most TV commercials are only 15 or 30 seconds long. Most people only remember one or two points from any conversation. Key in on short and think about the *one* thought you want someone to remember. Then make it "sticky" —something they will retain—by tying the thought to why it should matter to them—their WIIFM.

What to Say

Memorable elevator speeches include both a rational/intellectual component about the features of what you do and an emotional component [that answers the *why* and *what for*]. Good elevator speeches engage the whole brain. They awaken curiosity in the listener.

> A well-done elevator speech begins a conversation that leads to an opportunity to move the relationship further along. Begin with what you do [work features], then follow it with who it helps [benefits] *and* why it matters [value].

Consider what you do in terms of the customer's problems [WIIFM] and your solutions. Since the brain is trained by eons of experience to fixate on pain first, a focus on wrongs you can fix often helps people remember you. Some examples of work/benefits statements:

- Trust and estates lawyer: "Often people fight over inheritances. I craft inheritance documents [feature] that provide peace of mind for my clients [benefit] and give them a sense of control [benefit]. We create plans to distribute their assets according to their wishes [WIIFM]."
- Financial planner: "Divorce can lead to a more restricted life style. I show divorced women how to create a positive financial future [benefit] for themselves, and then work with them to implement their plan [WIIFM]."
- Patent attorney: "Don't you worry sometimes that someone will steal your idea? I help clients safeguard their intellectual property [benefit] by creating patents or trademarks [feature] to protect their ideas from the competition [WIIFM]. I also help them increase profits [WIIFM] by monetizing their patents [feature]."

People don't like to feel stupid, so when they encounter something they don't understand they tend to stop listening. To prevent this from happening, keep your sentences short and your language concise and jargon-free. Use

Worksheet 8.3 Elevator Speech Components, which you can find in Appendix 2, pages 198–199, to create your basic message.

Several interviewees shared their short, benefits-driven elevator speeches:

Bonnie Hagen, COO of Bright Energy Services, says, "Owners of commercial and industrial businesses [her target] save money [benefit] by saving on energy costs."[1] She doesn't begin with the technical details of the "how" and "what for" because her "why" is to help people conserve energy [WIIFM] and save money [WIIFM].

Lenny Carraturo, Wells Fargo middle market banking business development officer, says, "We help companies increase revenues, increase margins, and be more efficient [benefits]. How can we work together?" [WIIFM]. Then he asks about what the company they are discussing is doing in specific areas so he can segue to what the bank does.

Vikram Rajan, cofounder of PhoneBlogger.net, says, "You need to stay top of mind to get clients from word of mouth referrals." He tells them why his program [features] will increase their business and reputation [WIIFM], and only then does he explain how his company can make it happen more easily and for less money [benefits].

What to Convey

Your 30-second positioning infomercial should put into words something about you as a person. You want to show your intelligence, subject matter grasp, and, most importantly, enthusiasm about your job and the outcomes that you know you can achieve for your clients. Other features to communicate include:

- Confidence
- Passion
- Interest in others
- A track record of success
- A call to action

Basically, your brief speech encapsulates your positioning: the attributes you want people to associate with you.

1. Personal interview, September 7, 2017.

Practice Makes Perfect

To make an elevator speech sound natural, sincere, and unrehearsed takes hours of preparation. After you write it, practice it by reading it aloud and then saying it out loud in front of a mirror. Repeat until the words trip lightly off your tongue.

> Every client wants their service provider to exhibit three characteristics: in order of priority, availability, affability, and ability.

Then try it out on friends and family. When their eyes glaze over, you know you have a problem. When their eyes crinkle with excitement and they lean toward you, you have a winning proposition. When they can't wait to ask follow-up questions, you have a home run.

Once the basic text is a winner, create modified versions keyed to the concerns of different audiences. When new trends become apparent or new laws are enacted that will impact your clients' lives, amend your basic speech to keep it current. As you and your practice grow and evolve, your speech should reflect your changes. Think about the speech as an exercise written once but never finished.

Business Cards

A business card is your personal marketing introduction and leave-behind piece. When your card reflects you and your brand, it will remind people of their conversation with you. You want it to be memorable and stand out from the white paper/black ink pack. Your cards should reflect not only the "what" of your work but also the "why." Add a color or design that suits your personality. Add your differentiation tagline.

Other important business card requirements:

- Good paper stock. If you want to use gloss, limit it to one side so people can write notes on the other side.
- Legible type so it can be read by middle-aged people without their reading glasses.
- A line referring not only to what you are [your profession] but what you do [field of expertise] or, better yet, the benefits of what you do. This line is often the reason a card stands out in the sea of cards people take home. Examples:
  - If you consider LinkedIn an important networking tool, you should include your LinkedIn URL in your contact details
  - Patent attorney, wealth manager for millennials, forensic accountant and sleuth

    - Saver of dreams, advisor to decision makers, post-divorce financial planner
    - Results: saves money, offers protection, preserves assets
- Use both sides of the card, and put required but less immediately important information, such as street addresses and fax numbers, on the back.
- Remember to not fill every inch of the card. Leave space to set off the important parts of your text and for the card recipient to use in case s/he wants to take notes.

Sometimes you might want to reinforce your positive service approach and accessibility by handwriting something on your card such as your personal phone number or a reference to how much you enjoyed talking to them. Remember, if you include your mobile number, people will call it.

Sometimes you may want to offer a person two of your cards, saying, "You are such a good networker that I would like to give you two cards—one for you and one to give to one of your connections who you think should know me." Of course, the other person says "yes," giving you a chance to say thank you and reinforce why it is important to you.

A tip: Rather than fumble around looking for your cards, keep them separate and handy so you don't have to do the pocket patting routine.

Storytelling

Stories are a way to share knowledge. Short stories can be very powerful conveyors of the *how*, the *why*, and the *what for*. They show not only what you know but how you apply what you know and why doing what you do is important to you. Peter Guber, a film producer,[2] explained the business story this way:

> In business the story is told for an explicit purpose. You tell it to encourage the other person to see the value proposition you're offering, and to make that person want to be part of it. Without that story, you have only transactional elements and no relationships. Transactions happen only once; repeat business requires relationships. . . . The relationship element depends on purposeful storytelling.[3]

2. Peter Guber wrote *Tell to Win: Persuade and Triumph with the Hidden Power of Story*.
3. This quote is from an interview with him by Art Kleiner, "The Art of the Business Narrative," strategy-business.com, March 21, 2011, https://www.strategy-business.com/article/00067?gko=3e7b3.

Stories come in many versions:

- *The possible*: "Imagine you came home and found. . . ." or "You came in to work and found. . . ."
- *The actual*: "We were retained by a _________ to help them resolve a conflict with ______ that threatened to __________. Our approach was to _____________. The result was a savings of __________ for our client."
- *The theoretical*: "What do you think would happen to _________ if _______________?"

Good stories are everywhere. You can use myths, fables, ideas from books you've read, or generalize from daily work or life experiences. When the story is relevant and rings true for the audience, you've created a pathway linking them to you.

> At the chemical level, when we hear stories, our brains release oxytocin, the bonding hormone that causes us to really care about the people involved. . . . When you package [a point] as a story, your audience will be able to put themselves in your shoes connecting with your message on a personal, emotional level that will make them more likely to remember what you had to say, buy in to your ideas, and perceive you favorably.[4]

Stories can persuade and inspire people to accept cultural mores, take specific actions, follow certain leaders. They can break down physical and psychological barriers by creating visual images that relay the deeper messages we want others to hear and remember.

Sidebar 8.2 Storytelling: The Impact of a Good Story

A Story about Stubbornness: "Do your research, know your facts:

This is the transcript of a radio communication between a U.S. naval ship and a Canadian maritime agency off the coast of Newfoundland.

> *Americans: 'Please divert your course 15 degrees north to avoid a collision.'*
>
> *Canadians: 'Recommend you divert your course 15 degrees south to avoid collision.'*

4. Noah Zandan, "The Science of Stories: How Stories Impact Our Brains," https://www.quantifiedcommunications.com/blog/science-of-stories.

> *Americans: 'This is the captain of a U.S. Navy ship; I say again divert your course.'*
>
> *Canadians: 'I say again, you divert your course.'*
>
> *Americans: 'This is a United States aircraft carrier. We are accompanied by three destroyers, three cruisers, and numerous support vessels. I strongly request that you change your course 15 degrees north, that's one five degrees north, or we will be forced to take countermeasures to ensure the safety of this ship.'*
>
> *Canadians: 'We are a lighthouse; you make the call.'"*[5]

Most importantly, from a networking perspective, stories convey your authenticity, reinforce your expertise, and suggest that you are a practical and empathic person to work with. Telling stories that include a factual component with an emotional overlay turns your work with clients into something memorable. Stories are more believable than plain facts because they are grounded in real people with real problems that you resolved. When the story is appropriate to the audience, listeners will relate to it personally, applying the case scenario to events in their own lives or in the lives of people they know.

You can create stories from actual case studies by creating a composite of many situations to protect the confidentiality of specific clients. Good case studies contain three parts:

A beginning—the problem or opportunity
A middle—in general terms how you resolved it
The end—the result for the client

To be prepared for networking activities, you should have a handful of stories that illustrate your elevator speech points. Once you have integrated your target persona's qualities and your value proposition into your elevator speech and your powerful stories you are ready for any networking conversation. You have prepared a message that reflects the image you want to project.

Chapter Summary

In this chapter we talked about several networking "assists" that you can prepare ahead of time that will make it easier for you to convey your purpose in whatever networking venue you find yourself. The "assists" include:

5. Edward Wachtman and Sheree Johnson, StoryTelling™ Consulting, *The Persuasive Power of Story*, p. 2, http://www.storytellings.com/images/StoryTellings_Consulting_The_Persuasive_Power_of_Story.pdf.

- Target persona: an anthropomorphic abstraction that captures the characteristics, inclinations, interests, personality, and needs of your target client or referrer
- Your value proposition: why what you do is of value to your target
- Your elevator speech: a short introduction to your what, how, and why
- A business card that says "you"
- Your story—developing stories that bring home your message in a way that involves both the rational and emotional parts of your brain.

In addition to this pre-networking homework, you need to consider aspects of your performance that impact others' perception of you. When networking in-person, others will assess your presence and performance as indicators of how you would be if they worked with you. In the next chapter we talk about networking intangibles—attitude, body language, voice, conversation and listening skills—that are often more important than the words themselves.

Networking Preparation: Personal Intangibles 9

Personal intangibles—how you look, stand, smile, converse—matter. Often, body language is the key to being seen as warm versus soft, direct versus aggressive, authentic versus insincere. In fact, it is estimated that 93 percent of your impressions of someone are based on what you see. As shown in Figure 9.1, your body language alone represents 55 percent of what you communicate, your tone of voice 38 percent, and your words themselves only 7 percent.[1]

Figure 9.1 Communication Components

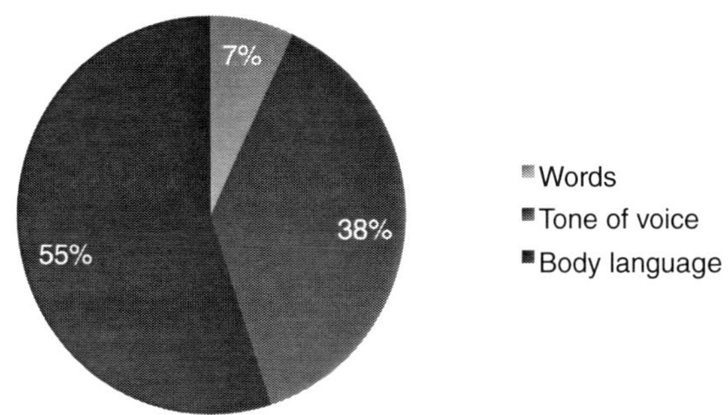

1. "Infographic: The Importance of Face to Face Networking," https://www.virgin.com/entrepreneur/infographic-importance-face-to-face-networking.

This may be why:

- "Nearly 100 percent of people say face-to-face meetings are essential for long-term business relationships."
- "Seventy-two percent of people say their impressions are impacted by how someone appears and their handshake."
- "68 percent of entry-level professionals value face-to-face networking more than online."[2]

Personal Intangibles

One of your most important networking assets is your personal brand. Your brand is a combination of these intangibles plus your goals, values, approach to life, and reputation. "Personal branding is nothing more than understanding what makes you interesting, compelling and differentiated and using that to stand out from your peers. It's about building a solid professional reputation around your unique promise of value."[3] Your brand connects you to people on the unconscious, emotional level by tying into the "why" you do what you do.

> Armanda C. Squadrilli, a top real estate broker, lives her brand: "I network my brand. If you want to be different, be significantly different and brand it."
>
> Marc W. Halpert, LinkedIn trainer, said, "Networking and your personal brand are linked. Writing, talking, teaching and client satisfaction are all part of networking and sharing your why [your brand]."

Think back to the emphasis in Chapter 2 on the "why" behind your work. In our brains, emotion always precedes cognitive thought. Your brand helps people relate at an emotional level to the authentic you before they ask for details about your work product. By learning to employ intangibles in a positive way, you will showcase your brand and enhance your confidence in successfully navigating any networking situation.

In this chapter we discuss two important intangibles—attitude and body language—and two ways in which these intangibles manifest themselves when you network—your visual image and conversation—both the content

2. All statistics from Aja Frost, "15 Surprising Stats on Networking and Face-to-Face Communication," https://blog.hubspot.com/sales/face-to-face-networking-stats.

3. Mack Collier, "How to Brand Yourself in a Competitive Job Market: Q&A with William Arruda," August 21, 2007, http://www.marketingprofs.com/7/brand-yourself-competitive-job-market-collier.asp.

and the style. Collectively these visible and invisible elements create your first impression.

The key components of personal intangibles are discussed in this chapter in the following sequence:

- Attitude
- Visual image, including
  - Posture
  - Deportment—the way a person behaves
  - Clothing/colors
- Body language, including
  - Facial expressions
  - Breathing
  - Proxemics—the process of indicating how you feel by the way you place your body in relation to others
  - Gestures, including touch
- Conversation skills
  - Small talk
  - Active and attentive listening

Together, these elements create the image you present to others. People make initial snap judgments of others almost instantly. They trust their insights, so it is often difficult to change their minds. As the power of seven suggests, it is far better to pay attention to that first impression and make sure it is the one you want others to notice.

Power of Seven

Seven seconds to make a first impression.

Seven initiatives to overcome a bad one.

Seven contacts before someone remembers you.

Seven contacts a year to stay top of mind with people who know you.

Attitude

The most important personal networking attributes are psychological. Attitude matters more than aptitude. Anyone, even introverts and recluses, can learn to be comfortable by using the strategic networking process to create a safe environment. Going through the preparation process lets networkers feel comfortably prepared for any activity.

This comfort level gives them sufficient confidence to step a bit outside themselves and concentrate on those they meet. The key to networking is not whether you are happy at parties. It is your interest in other people. Ellen Volpe, facilitator-owner of American Business Associates Groups, says the key to effectiveness is your attitude: "A willingness to be interested in other people."

The interviewees all agreed that no one likes to be sold to. People who shy away from networking tend to equate networking with sleazy car salespeople looking to overwhelm you with information you don't want about something you would never buy. And, of course, some networkers come across this way. But, as we've discussed, networking is not about selling what you have. It is about finding out what others need and then helping them to reach their goals. If the path to their goals requires your skill set, you may get work.

When you demonstrate a sincere interest in other people—what they do, why they do it, where your interests overlap, how you can help them achieve their goals—you are perceived as a "giver" rather than a "getter." When you embrace the giver mentality, your attitude intangibly conveys this feeling. People sense a subtle congruity between your words and image that reinforces your authenticity.

David Rosenbaum, creator of several networking groups, put it succinctly: "[In WBN] we're not allowed to sell to each other, even though many of us buy from each other. None of us wants to walk into a room full of salespeople trying to sell us something. Buying from each other represents a very different transaction. Who wouldn't want to buy from someone they've come to know and trust."

Larry Hutcher, co-managing partner of Davidoff, Hutcher & Citron, never asks anyone for a piece of business. His attitude is one of helping. He is a thoughtful listener and an outstanding people connector; always thinking how his resources and referral network can help someone else. He is happy to advise or fill requests for introductions concerning almost any problem or opportunity regardless of whether they relate to business or personal issues. He feels that while paying it forward is its own reward, often it turns into work because people he has helped think of him when a legal need arises.

Steven Spielvogel, lawyer and creator of the international networking group INBLF, says that good networkers are successful people who have an ability to be naturally very social so others enjoy being around them. At the same time, they bring along something of value, including an attitude of helpfulness that is useful to others. Good networkers support other peoples' efforts to move toward what is important to them.

Image

Appearance matters. According to a recent survey:

- Eighty percent of the respondents agreed that "everyone judges other people's looks."[4]
- "64 percent of people said that the first thing they notice about someone is how attractive he or she is."[5]
- "And half of us—that's every *other person*—think appearance defines us significantly or completely."[6]

Authentic images are powerful. People believe in them because they come across as real, genuine, and appropriate.

The word "image" has many definitions, but three are appropriate here:

- A representation or likeness of a person or thing
- A mental representation or picture; idea produced by the imagination
- The personality presented to the public by a person, organization, etc.[7]

You create your image from a combination of presence, deportment, body language, and clothing.

Posture: Posture creates presence. Learn to "stand tall," with your feet slightly apart and placed under your hips and your hands comfortably at your side. This imparts a sense of command or control.

> [T]he most important benefit good posture confers is chemical. When you stand tall, feet planted solidly and somewhat apart, chest out and shoulders back, you actually trigger a hormonal response that boosts testosterone and lowers cortisol.[8]

> "Posture creates presence."

When seated, continue to project professionalism by sitting upright. To stay upright naturally place your backside against the back of the chair, balance on your "sitting bones and lean forward slightly toward the conversation. Again,

---

4. Danielle Pergament, "Exactly How Much Appearance Matters, According to Our National Judgment Survey," February 10, 2016, https://www.allure.com/story/national-judgement-survey-statistics?verso=true
5. Ibid.
6. Ibid.
7. All three definitions come from the British Dictionary, http://www.dictionary.com/browse/image?s=t.
8. Sylvia Ann Hewlett, *EP Executive Presence* (HarperCollins, 2014), p. 71.

you will project a sense of energy, interest and confidence. To radiate presence, you have to radiate that you *are* present."[9]

Deportment: Deportment, the manner in which you behave, matters. When you are introduced, hold out your hand, look in the person's eyes, smile, and shake hands firmly. This immediately conveys approachability, authority, and attention. Continue to pay attention to the person you are talking to. People who converse with one eye out for the next opportunity signal insincerity and disinterest.

Use an understanding of business etiquette to underscore your image. For example, cell phones and similar devices should be turned off at networking events, unless you expect an urgent call. If you have to leave the device on, be sure to silence it, using vibrate to let you know that calls have arrived. Do not put the phone on the table—even face down. To leave a cell phone on and visible during conversations creates an image that contradicts an attentive attitude and body language.

Clothing and Colors

Clothing: Clothing is a signal as to your intentions and your gravitas. "When you make an effort to look polished, you signal to others that you see them as worth your time and investment."[10] Your choice of clothing should reflect the event and the attendees; but you should always look put together. "Your appearance should focus your audience on your professional competencies, not distract from them."[11]

In some instances, there is a preconceived notion as to what you should wear. Many assume that successful lawyers, accountants, and bankers wear suits or, at minimum, a sports jacket. Similarly, what we see on television and in the news tells us that techies wear hoodies and casual clothes. It is your personal call as to whether you conform to the stereotypes or not. Just be sure to consider the impact of whichever choice you make.

Be comfortable. It is uncomfortable for others to watch someone fiddling with their clothes. At an event you may be standing for long periods of time so, of course, comfortable footwear is a must. Meeting room weather is as variable as outside; layers can make a difference. Often, women carry scarves for protection when the air conditioning soars.

Pay as much attention to your looks as others do. Wear the highest quality clothing you can afford, invest in a good tailor, and be judicious in your use of perfume and jewelry.

9. Ibid.
10. Ibid., p. 84.
11. Ibid., p. 87.

Color: "Color is an important form of nonverbal communication."[12] Most colors have many meanings. The specific meaning will vary depending on the setting, your mood, and the response color elicits in others. For example, if you want to stand out at a meeting wear a bright color to signal your intention. If you want to be seen as safe and friendly wear blue or green—two colors that connote trust and calm.

- "Blue is the color of trust and peace. It can suggest loyalty and integrity as well as conservatism and frigidity."
- "Green is the color of balance and growth. It can mean both self-reliance as a positive and possessiveness as a negative."[13]

Color associations, like body language, are learned through cultural norms and personal experience. For example, red is the color for weddings in India and white is the color of mourning. In America, we marry in white and wear black for mourning.

Body Language

Body language is partially innate and partially learned. It can be defined as "nonverbal, usually unconscious, communication through the use of postures, gestures, facial expressions, and the like."[14] Body language includes:

- Facial expressions
- Breathing
- Proxemics—the process of indicating how you feel by the way you place your body in relation to others
- Gestures, including touch

Micro Expressions

"Never underestimate the communicative power of body language . . . [Y]our body language and poise are what they see first."[15] Your attitude is telegraphed in microseconds through your body language. Our micro signals constantly show how we really feel.

> Micro expressions are facial expressions that occur within 1/25th of a second. They are involuntary and expose a person's true emotions. . . .

12. From "Understanding the Meaning of Color in Color Psychology," http://www.empower-yourself-with-color-psychology.com/meaning-of-colors.html.
13. Ibid. The article lists the primary meanings of basic colors.
14. Dictionary.com Unabridged, Based on the Random House Dictionary, © Random House, Inc. 2018.
15. Sylvia Ann Hewlett, p. 69.

> Everyone flashes micro expressions and no one can hide them. . . . All around the globe we express the same seven universal emotions. They include: anger, fear, sadness, disgust, surprise, contempt, and happiness.[16]

When we spot incongruence between micro signals—a mouth twitch, an eyebrow raised, pupils contracted—and the rest of someone's body language, we unconsciously feel uncomfortable. If asked, we would say that the other person seems insincere, artificial, or fake.

> "Jeffrey A. Blutstein, a financial advisor, says, 'The greatest networkers are con men or genius salesmen because they have a talent for picking up micro signals. They have highly honed levels of awareness and observation so they see nuances that others miss.'"

You can learn to control some aspects of the way you appear to others through self-awareness and self-control. However, you never can control everything about your body language. That's why I say: "People lie, bodies don't." As Amy B. Goldsmith advises, "Do what makes you comfortable. Otherwise your body language gives you away."

When there is congruence between our verbal language and body language, it can be as powerful and beautiful as when 36 Rockettes kick their legs in unison. When Rockette Alissa LaVergne was asked if newcomers were hazed her answer illustrated the importance of micro signals. She said: "We are all in it together. If you don't have that camaraderie and we don't have that bond, it will show onstage."[17] The 'it" in this case would be the micro expressions of individuality that would subconsciously mar their image of perfect precision.[18]

16. "Micro Expressions," https://www.paulekman.com/micro-expressions/. See also, "How to Detect Micro Expressions" updated September 26, 2017, https://bizfluent.com/how-5311172-detect-micro-expressions.html.

17. Mark Kennedy, "Secrets of the Rockettes Revealed," The Journal News, p. 13A (December 3, 2017).

18. https://www.rockettes.com/blog/fun-facts-about-the-radio-city-christmas-spectacular-and-the-rockettes/.

Smiles and Eyes: Two of the most important positive body language properties are your eyes and your smile. We take smiles for granted and rarely think about how they seem to others.

Smiles: Genuine, sincere smiles signify happiness, acceptance, and confidence. Smiles are generated by the unconscious brain when we feel pleasure: The mouth muscles move up at the corners, the cheeks rise, the forehead wrinkles, the eyes light up and narrow [your laugh lines], and the eyebrows dip slightly.

Insincere smiles occur when a smile is required, but the person is not in a happy situation. At such times we consciously make our mouths smile by moving our mouth muscles; the rest of the face doesn't respond. As the recipient of such a smile you immediately feel the disconnect and sense something is fake.

Smiles can also signal reward, affiliation, and dominance, which we respond to.

- "The dominant smile is mildly lopsided, with closed lips and one or both eyes squeezed shut,
- "Whereas reward smiles show upturned lips exposing a row of teeth and crinkled eyes.
- "Affiliation smiles feature pursed lips, the whites of the eyes and raised eyebrows."[19]

Eyes: Eyes are said to be a window to your soul. In the context of body language, eyes regulate conversation and, along with smiles, give cues as to dominance in a relationship.

> Over the course of conversation, eye contact is made through a series of glances—by the speaker, to make sure the other person has understood or to gauge reactions and by the listener, to indicate interest. . . . It is also used as a synchronizing signal. A person tends to look up at the end of utterances, which gives the listener warning that the speaker is about to stop talking.[20]

> As Marc W. Halpert, LinkedIn trainer, explained it, 'Eye contact is an essential part of your personal vocabulary. Looking at people when you are conversing shows you are following the discussion and that you are present.'

19. Susan Pinker, "Mind & Matter: A Smile's Many Messages—Some Unfriendly," *Wall Street Journal*, April 7–8, 2018.
20. Carol Kinsey Goman, *The Nonverbal Advantage: Secrets and Science of Body Language at Work*, 2008, pp. 43–44.

Eye contact, smiling, proximity, and most other body language cues are culturally determined. Here we are assuming the American context. Should you network in other countries or speak with foreign-born audiences you should research their body language and try to manage your own body language appropriately. For example, Americans see eye contact as an indication of interest and attention; while in Asian cultures avoiding direct eye contact can be a sign of respect and deference.

Mirroring: People like, trust, and relate better to people who seem to be like them. The body, often unconsciously, uses "mirroring" techniques to create compatibility and comfort in a group. Mirroring refers to the natural process of matching the behavior of others by adopting their mannerisms, such as their speech cadence, gestures, sitting or standing positions, etc.

For example, in meetings, people tend to adopt the body position of the group's leaders. Or, when speaking, if the lead speaker's cadence is slower than yours, your speech will normally unconsciously slow down. Often women appear at a meeting wearing similar outfits—mirroring.

Mirroring signals nonverbally that we like or agree with the other person. In networking, mirroring fosters mutual rapport. Noicing these signals when you are networking offers clues as to whether or not you want to join a conversation.

Breathing: Regular breathing signals confidence. When the body takes in more oxygen it increases your ability to think and your whole stance and attitude become more positive. Conversely, when a person is stressed they may take deep breaths or pant because the body is trying to increase its oxygen intake as part of its unconscious "fight or flight" response. Shallow breathing suggests low confidence or anxiety. Since it is common for people in groups to adopt the breathing rhythm of those around them, a shallow breather can make everyone near them anxious.[21]

Proxemics: Proxemics is defined as "the study of the symbolic and communicative role in a culture of spatial arrangements and variations in distance, as in how far apart individuals engaged in conversation stand depending on the degree of intimacy between them."[22] This physical distance between individuals is culturally and situationally determined. For example, people who live in crowded areas, such as cities, are culturally conditioned to a greater degree of closeness.

Everyone lives in their own bubble, which varies in size depending on context and gender. Experts say the following are optimum proximities for most Americans:

- 1 to 18 inches: intimate space between lovers, parents and children, close friends, people and their pets

21. Ibid.
22. Dictionary.com.

- 18 inches to 4 feet: work space or events/situations where you know most of the people
- 4 to 12 feet: nontouch distance between people we don't know or don't know well, e.g., strangers, repairmen, queues
- 12+ feet: public areas with no interaction, such as sidewalks[23]

Women tend to stand closer to one another, face each other more, and touch each other more than men do.

These distances probably sound impossibly far apart for people who work in corporate settings, commute to work or live in big cities. Yet we know these spaces are unconsciously important to us when we feel uncomfortably crowded at cocktail parties by the lack of sufficient space.

Another in-person situation impacted by proxemics relates to the cohesion of groups. How does someone outside a group and wanting to join them figure out whether the group is open to expansion? One way is to see if they are close together and leaning toward each other—two signs that they are engaged.

Feet offer important cues as to what someone else is thinking or feeling. Since prehistoric times, the direction of one's feet has signaled where we want to go.[24] For example,

- We point our lead foot in the direction the mind wants to go whether it be toward the most attractive person or toward the exit.
- Jiggling feet indicate the brain's inclination to run away.
- When looking to join a conversation, watch the group members' feet. "If the feet of your two colleagues stay in place, and they twist only their upper torsos in your direction, they don't really want you to join the conversation. If they are willing to include you the foot nearest you will turn slightly in your direction."[25]

Touch: Touch is a way to indicate that you want to be in a closer relationship with the other person. Among the most important networking touches is the handshake. A handshake is your first physical contact

"We point our lead foot in the direction the mind wants to go whether it be toward the most attractive person or toward the exit."

23. Allan and Barbara Pease, *The Definitive Book of Body Language* (Bantam Books, 2006) pp. 194–196.
24. Carol Kinsey Goman, *The Nonverbal Advantage: Secrets and Science of Body Language at Work*, 2008, p. 105.
25. Ibid., p. 109.

with another person. It should convey your image as a trusted, knowledgeable professional.

For an effective handshake, take a small step forward, firmly grasp the other person's hand, look them in the eye, smile a genuine smile, shake intentionally but not excessively, and say hello. This is not hand wrestling, nor is it a "limp fish" convention. It is a "tribal ritual" that creates a first brief physical connection to another person.

Business cards: Another touch event is often overlooked at American networking events—the business card exchange. Typically, we ask for a card and then pocket it without looking at it. Instead, make it another symbol of your interest in creating a relationship by holding the card in two hands, reading it and commenting on some aspect.

For example,

- "I didn't know Donald was your middle name. Were you named for your father?"
- "Looking at your card reminds me of a contact who might be a useful referral source for you. I will make an introduction."
- "You and _______ are in the same field but at different size firms. Do you know him? Would you like me to introduce you?"

This reinforces the message of your handshake, and the full attention attitude you want to communicate. The act of really focusing on the card when you receive it will help you to remember the person's name, but more importantly, by showing that you value your interaction with this person, you will become memorable to him/her.[26]

Reading Body Language

Your audience forms many immediate ideas about you, inferring them from how you move, speak, and interact with them. Your networking posture, deportment, body language, and attitude create an expectation that you will act the same way if you are hired. Poor posture, weak handshake, slapdash appearance taken together distract from your professionalism. Confident body language indicated by your image, focused attention, and genuine interest in other people all evoke a feeling of confidence in others.

Reading body language requires an understanding of the context. Body language will differ by age, gender, country of origin, and the situation itself. Are you at a bar association meeting or a bar? A ball game or a community meeting?

Generally, you look for at least three complementary signs to intuit how another person is feeling. If you are rubbing your eyes, are they dry or are you

26. See a fuller discussion of business cards in Chapter 8, 111–112.

upset? If your arms are crossed, are you cold or defensive? If you scratch your nose, are you lying or does it itch?

Several signs of hostility, negativity, or lying include:

- Critical or negative thinking is indicated by the thumb supporting the chin while the index finger points up along the cheek. Or sometimes, the person combines a chin stroke with crossed arms and legs and leans back in the chair.
- Hands behind a person's back signals "back away."
- Hostility to you or your conversation is indicated by several behaviors, including when a person's legs and arms are tightly crossed, when the head and chin are tilted down, and/or when a person sits back rather than leans forward.[27]

Body language can signal a person's degree of interest in a conversation or participation in decision making. For example,

- You can infer genuine interest when the person's hand rests under the chin but is not used for support. Or, when they stroke their chin and lean forward or gesture with open arms. Other signs of interest include nodding your head or tilting it to one side.
- When a person's head rests on one hand, chances are s/he is bored.
- When someone chews on a pencil or plays with paperclips while a discussion is going on they are probably undecided.
- Open/uncrossed legs indicate a dominant position or open attitude. Open arms or arms akimbo indicate the same.
- Closed/crossed legs suggest closed attitudes or uncertainty.[28]

Sight is our dominant sense, so consider your behavioral message carefully. As Figure 9.1 shows, 55 percent of communication is visual. Learn to be mindful of your body's message and use your intangibles to reinforce your verbal messages. At the same time, be mindful of the potentially negative impact of body language when you are tired, sad, depressed, or just uncomfortable. If you can't overcome these feelings, you may want to stay home rather than go to an event and have your image work against you.

To maximize your network effect, take time before an activity to put yourself in a positive, outgoing frame of mind. People like people who project confidence, seem in a good mood, and are enthusiastic. "Making others feel good increases your appeal."[29]

---

27. Carol Kinsey Goman, *The Nonverbal Advantage: Secrets and Science of Body Language at Work*, 2008, chapter 5.

28. Ibid.

29. David J. Lieberman, "Instant Rapport: The Secrets of Likability," *Bottom Line Personal*, June 1, 2000.

Alla Roytberg summed it up, "Be present with people. It all goes back to attitude, showing others that you genuinely care and want to help them."

Amy B. Goldsmith put it another way, "People can see integrity through your intentions."

Jeffrey A. Blutstein is a financial advocate but his favorite networking location is on the golf course where he is most comfortable. "When he uses golf as a networking venue, he notes the chemistry while they play and if it feels good, he follows up with them in a business setting. It may seem incongruous to infer an interest in working together from a golf stance. Jeff's answer is: "Expertise is transferable. It is all about perception. If you are good at one thing, then people think you are good at other things."

Jeffrey also finds that "If a person can take time off during the week to play golf, he likely has the money for equipment and fees, and the time control we seek in leads. So golf leads to a self-winnowing and sifting of people with money and a need to buy what we sell."

Conversation

Most people like to talk about themselves and their lives. This has led to a marketing rule of thumb: God gave you two ears and one mouth so you could talk one-third of the time and listen two-thirds of the time.

Think of conversation as a collaborative team sport where the goal is to toss the conversational gambit from one person to another, listening all the while and thinking about ways to help the other person score a goal.[30]

Ask open-ended questions to encourage the other person to talk about him/herself. Examples of closed and open-ended questions include:

- *Closed*: Did you go to Smith College?
- Open: What did you like most about your college experience?
- *Closed*: Do you like working for [person's name] or at [firm name]?
- Open: What aspects of your work are most interesting to you?

As you listen to the other person's answers, you will form a picture of her/him, note overlapping interests, and find areas where you can help.

There are two types of conversations: small talk and focused or agenda-driven conversation.

- *Small talk* is often equated with chitchat about unimportant, noncontroversial topics such as the weather, sports, food, travel, children. But it

30. Jayne Navarre, response on an LMA egroup, January 21, 2010.

can also be an entry-point into a deeper discussion with a new contact. Regardless of its substance, small talk is a social lubricant. Sometimes it may lead to more content-rich conversation; other times it will ease your passage through a room full of people you don't know, don't remember, or haven't seen in a long time.

- *Agenda-driven conversation* is a key component of the strategic network planning that should occur prior to any specific networking activity [as discussed in Chapter 10, pages 141–145]. In these conversations, you are looking for commonalities in terms of interests, activities, aspirations and ways to help and be helped.

Small Talk: Small talk is a practice that can create meaningful, valuable exchanges between strangers who have never met before or people who are reconnecting. It can also reinforce your position as a member of a group. "'Mastering the banter' [i.e., small talk] shows that you're part of the larger conversation, someone who's 'one of the tribe.'" As a group member you have knowledge to share in casual conversations. You are just "one of the boys."[31]

Many people dislike networking because they think it is all small talk, which they define as boring chatter with relative strangers. Even in a new networking environment, small talk doesn't have to be banal, dreary, or useless. It can be a way to begin interesting conversations that provide insight into the person you are talking to. "We should consider it [small talk] the appetizer for every relationship. It can turn a challenging, awkward situation into a success. Small talk connects us and helps us build relationships whether the setting is business or social."[32]

Bonnie Hagen, COO of an energy company, said she likes small talk because "it is a way to find something in common" and it reinforces her belief that "everyone has value."

Armanda C. Squadrilli, real estate broker, says it is "very important to immediately find a point of connection or rapport. It helps to know a little bit about a lot of things because it makes it easier to find that connection."

The secret is simple. Boring small talk tends to resemble a tit-for-tat conversation where one person makes a statement and the other person responds with the equivalent answer about themselves. If, instead of verbal ping pong, you challenge the other person with an interesting question, you create the

31. Sylvia Ann Hewlett, EP Executive Presence, p. 68.

32. Debra Fine, "Make the Most of Mingling," RIPit!, *Law Practice Magazine*, November/December 2003, p. 64.

opportunity for an unexpected conversation and the chance to seem memorable enough to be remembered.

Unusual, unexpected, personal questions immediately spark attention in the unsuspecting other person who was waiting to be asked why he was at the event or what he does for a living. It tunes into our emotional response mechanism, which unconsciously makes us happier. And it can lead to valuable exchanges in which you discover unusual details about other people. Some simple examples:

- Instead of "What do you do?" ask "What was the most interesting thing you did today?" or "What do like best about your job?" or "Why did you become a [put in their profession]?"
- If the talk turns to travel, instead of saying "I've been to Paris too," ask "What was the most exciting thing you did while you were there?" or "How do you let go of work stress on vacation?" or "What three places are on your travel wish list?"
- Instead of commenting on the weather, reference the day's weather by asking how the other person likes to spend his/her time when it [rains/snows/is hot].
- Use the classic six-word open-ended question: "What keeps you up at night?"
- Or the classic five-word networking question: "How can I help you?"

> "Asking probing questions is a perfect way for shy people or introverts to put the spotlight on the other person. Introverts tend to prefer meaningful conversations with a few people rather than chitchat with millions."

"The ability to draw others into meaningful conversations can determine whether people want to get to know you or remember you at all."[33]

Often, introverts are more comfortable taking the time to probe more deeply into a small talk topic. Asking probing questions is a perfect way to put the spotlight on the other person.

> Small talk might seem like a way to stay professional in business settings by avoiding overly personal topics. But the truth is, when it comes to networks, business is better when it is personal. . . . Better connections come from deeper conversations. And those deeper conversations are more welcomed by introverts. So while they may not feel like working the room, introverts may be better networkers over the long term than

33. Sue Shellenbarger, "Save Yourself from Tedious Small Talk," *Wall Street Journal*, May 24, 2017.

their extroverted counterparts precisely because they don't "work the room." Instead, they stick to just a few conversations and go deeper.[34]

Vocal Tone: Tone is an important part of image. People expect professionals to speak clearly and with energy, in a well-modulated tone. You want to use voice inflection and intonation to help your audience understand your meaning. Also vary the speed at which you speak. If you want others to be excited, first be excited yourself. These emotions move through groups.

Remember, it takes only seconds to form an opinion about someone, so be especially careful to state your name clearly. Don't be afraid to ask someone to repeat their name or even to spell it. People like to be told that their name is "pretty," or asked to explain the derivation of an unusual name.

Don't use jargon unless you are talking with someone else in your profession. Jargon, whether it be legalese, financial data argot, or accounting terminology, is an insider's shortcut. It can feel exclusionary and patronizing to outsiders. When others don't understand you, it creates a disconnect that cuts the rapport you are seeking to establish. Not understanding can make people feel stupid or uninformed, so they cease to listen.

When you begin to speak, choose affirmative words that reinforce your positive attitude. When you are talking, lose filler words, especially "uhm" and "like," or the millennials' favorite, "awesome." Instead signal the end of sentences with silence. Your audience doesn't need noise to connect your points. In fact, a bit of silence after a sentence allows them to catch up with your spoken thoughts.

Sometimes when people are nervous they tend to monopolize a conversation, extending a point beyond listeners' interest. Try to limit your end of the conversation to short sentences and paragraphs so you can throw the conversational ball to others.

Sidebar 9.2 Speaking Do's and Don'ts

Do speak in a clear, modulated tone.

Do try to frame comments in a positive way, because being positive or negative reflects back on the speaker.

34. David Burkus, "Why Introverts Might Actually Be Better Networkers," May 14, 2018, https://work.qz.com/1277113/networking-events-why-introverts-might-actually-be-better-at-them/.

Don't mumble.

Don't let your voice go up at the end of declarative statements as if you were questioning what you just said.

Don't let sentences drop off at the end. Instead, pause between thoughts to let listeners catch up with you. Pausing also suggest command of your language and thoughts, which unconsciously reinforces an expectation of competence.

Do adjust your conversation to your audience. Jargon is fine if you are conversing with peers. It is off-putting if used with people who might not understand it. Remember to nonlawyers, a tort is a cake.

Don't use filler words like "uhm" or "like." They are the mind's way of marking time. They create unnecessary hitches for listeners trying to follow your reasoning.

Listening

Listening is an important technique for establishing rapport. When you practice "active listening" you will be able to help others more successfully because you will hear what they want more clearly.

"Active listening" means, as its name suggests, actively listening. That is fully concentrating on what is being said rather than just passively "hearing" the message of the speaker.

Active listening involves listening with all senses. As well as giving full attention to the speaker, it is important that the "active listener" is also "seen" to be listening—otherwise the speaker may conclude that what they are talking about is uninteresting to the listener.

Interest can be conveyed to the speaker by using both verbal and non-verbal messages such as maintaining eye contact, nodding your head and smiling, agreeing by saying 'Yes' or simply 'Mmm hmm' to encourage them to continue.[35]

Stephen Covey, author of *The 7 Habits of Highly Effective People*, suggests that people learn what he calls "empathic listening." He says: "Most people do not listen with intent to understand. They listen with intent to reply. . . . In empathic listening you listen with your ears, but also with your eyes and with your heart."[36] You focus on the other person's emotional message behind the words.

You can demonstrate active listening in several ways:

- Use your understanding of body language to show your engagement. Face the speaker and mirror or complement their body language.

35. https://www.skillsyouneed.com/ips/active-listening.html.
36. Quoted in Virginia Johnson, "Listening with Empathy," *Successful Meetings* (March 1993, pp. 122–123).

- Begin your response to their thoughts by summarizing what you heard and what you think it means, using some of their words and phrases, and then ask them to corroborate the correctness of your assessment.
- Focus your attention on them for two reasons.
  - You need to pay attention in order to fully understand both the verbal and intangible aspects of what the person wants to communicate.
  - By paying attention only to them, you make the other person feel special. The secret to Bill Clinton's and Jackie Kennedy's charisma was an ability to give all their attention to whomever they were speaking with, leaving the other person feeling that for those 30 seconds they had been bathed in a special and personal relationship.

If you're not convinced of the merits of active listening, bear in mind that "true listening may feel like it slows you down, but in the end, it saves time because it results in fewer mistakes and misunderstandings that have to be rectified."[37]

Chapter Summary

Mark Bowden summarizes the importance of intangibles well:

> We all leave behind something in every interaction that we have. . . . Every time you interact and communicate, you create and leave behind ripples in the ponds of a great many individual perceptions, emanating out across time and space from the point of interaction. Well after you physically leave any one interaction, the experience of your legacy lives on in the way others react to you, what they think and feel about you, what they are going to do with the message they received from you, and to what extent they feel energized and inspired to work along with you.[38]

When you combine your prepared networking tools and your value proposition with confidence that you will be aware of the messages your body sends and receives, you are ready to excel at networking activities as discussed in Chapter 10.

37. John Mattone, Blog, "Why Listening Tops the Chart of Leadership Skills," https://johnmattone.com/2017/12/, December 20, 2017.

38. Mark Bowden, *Winning Body Language* (McGraw-Hill Books, 2010), p. 60.

The Three-Part Networking Implementation Strategy 10

Effective strategic networking is a three-stage process. The previous chapters are all prelude to your actual involvement in networking activities. You have created goals and goal strategies; selected off-line and online participation venues; prepared your communication tools, such as your elevator speech; and taken control of your body language and communication sound bites. Now it will all come together. In this chapter we look at best practices for making yourself comfortable and effective in networking situations. Go forth and conquer!

First, Let's Go Back to the Beginning

Yogi Berra knew that "if you don't know where you are going, you'll end up someplace else."[1] Networking without pre-meeting preparation and post-meeting follow-up is not strategic; it is just a random act of lunch.

Before you can plan for any specific event you need to review your strategies and goals [as outlined in Chapter 2]. Where you network and with whom will depend on your answers to these kinds of questions.

- Is your client base consumer oriented or individual oriented? [B2C] or some of both? If B2C or both you may want to join some of the mixed general networking groups.
- Is your client base focused on companies, organizations, businesses? [B2B]? If only B2B you may want to focus on profession-only groups or professional or industry/trade associations. If you are looking for a specific kind of business, find them on LinkedIn, in mixed membership groups, industry/trade associations, or civic associations.

1. Michelle Gorman, "Yogi Berra's Most Memorable Sayings," September 23, 2015, http://www.newsweek.com/most-memorable-yogi-isms-375661.

- Are you looking for referrals from colleagues? A logical place to begin is in your professional associations or law school alumni associations.
- Are you a young professional just starting in practice? Begin with alumnae associations, professional associations, and community-based groups.
- Are you an experienced networker? You may want to create your own private group and/or focus on mastermind networking meetings where you will share ideas and advice with others who have similar business issues and networking goals.

Once you have joined appropriate groups and begin to attend their meetings, you will need to refresh and refocus your general plan to maximize your return on each specific event. Every time you begin an activity, begin by answering the following questions:

- Basic questions always:
  - Who am I targeting here?
  - Why am I targeting them?
  - What are the significant characteristics of this group that are relevant to my goals?
- This specific activity:
  - How does this activity move me toward my goals?
  - Are there any specific attendees I would like to meet or be introduced to?
  - Do I know anyone who will be attending this activity?
  - Should I invite others to join me? If so, from which part of my networks?
  - How can I deliver value to people in this audience?
  - What should be the emphasis in my elevator speech?
  - What can I learn from the meeting speaker, topic, and/or attendees?
  - What results do I want from this networking opportunity?
  - Can I help the people I talk to move toward where they want to go?

Keeping these answers in mind, look at the range of possible networking opportunities and select a handful to pursue. Don't jump into too many activities at once. Better to select carefully and fully explore the opportunities offered by each selection before moving to the next one.

Bonnie Hagen, COO of Bright Energy Services, is on the board of the UJA Westchester Business and Professional Group. She tells a story that illustrates the importance of aligning goals and networking activities.

- She joined the UJA board because she was impressed by the power of the people in the room to raise money and mobilize resources quickly. She says this board is her favorite because it "helps everyone everywhere" and is also "good for business networking."

- She immediately became active on a committee and is now co-chair of a special needs program subcommittee.
- As chair, she was invited to a fundraiser for a special needs children's camp.
- She was then invited on a UJA leaders tour of the camp.
- While walking around the camp she noticed a need for solar lighting.
- She offered advice.
- This led to an introduction to members of the UJA Manhattan Real Estate Division, which will likely lead to work for her company.
- Bonnie would agree that "what goes around, comes around."

Time Considerations

Networking takes time. Time to plan, time to implement, time to evaluate. As you begin to select venues and join groups with monthly or semi-monthly meetings think about the time. There is no point in committing to any online or offline activity if you cannot calendar the time to actually do it well.

- Pre-event activities can take anywhere from half-an-hour to one and one-half hours depending on how much you already know about the organization and its members. If you are an active member you may only need half an hour to identify who you want to meet and connect with them ahead of time. If it is a new activity it will take longer to understand its potential.
- At the activity plus transportation to and from time can take anywhere from three to four and a half hours.
- Post-activity follow-up best practices, like pre-event best practices, can take anywhere from half an hour to an hour and one-half depending upon your familiarity with the group (Figure 10.1).

Total time per activity can run anywhere from four and one-half hours to seven and a half hours. If time pressures force you to skimp on or skip the pre- or post-networking activities, you will benefit less from the event.

Figure 10.1 Three-Phase Implementation Time Allotment

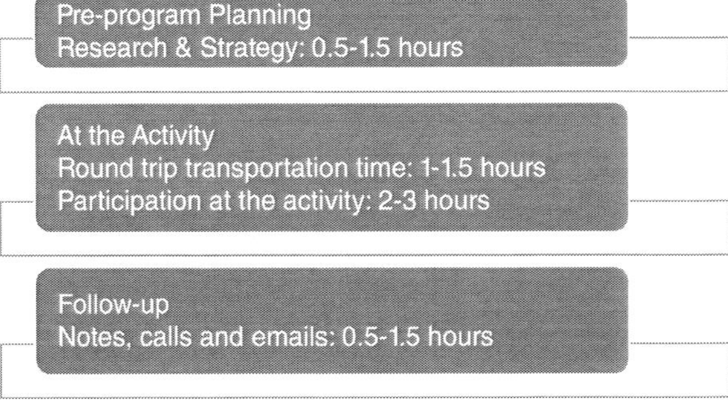

Three Stages of Implementation

Once you have chosen activities it is time to implement your strategy by using the three-part approach to specific networking interactions as shown in Figure 10.2.

- *Stage 1. Pre-activity*: Research about the group, the people, the topic, in order to have in mind key points to use in personal conversations at the event and to identify individuals you want to connect with at the event.
- *Stage 2. Actual event activity*: A set of behaviors that will enhance the occasion for you, and maximize your successful execution of your decision to participate.
- *Stage 3. Post-event activity*: Updates to your contact database, next steps that follow logically from whatever happened at this activity, and an analysis of what worked, what didn't work, plus ideas for improvements for next time.

Figure 10.2 Three Stages of Networking Implementation

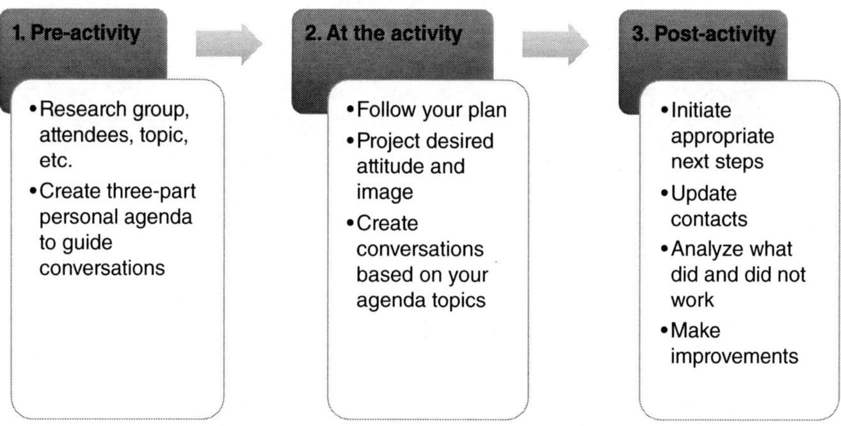

As we highlight the key actions at each stage think about how you want to adapt this basic model to fit your own style and activities. Use Worksheet 10.1 Pre- and Post-Activity Worksheet to help you prepare.

Interviewees have various approaches to how they choose a venue, whom they want to meet, and which services they want to highlight.

Steven Spielvogel, lawyer and founder of INBLF group, says that at meetings he "is laser-focused on specific individuals he wants to meet. In this regard, it is helpful to know what you are looking for and what you want from your networking." He prefers one good connection with someone you want to know rather than random conversations with a multitude of attendees.

Marcia Sloman, a professional organizer, focuses her networking on therapists for two reasons. One, she finds that their clients' problems often manifest physically as organization issues, such as hoarding or disorganization. Second, she prefers connecting with people who want deeply personal relationships with people "who get you, who really take the time to know you and what makes you tick."

Alla Roytberg, a matrimonial attorney and mediator, highlights different services in her different groups. For instance, in professional groups, "I pitch complementary services" such as her international divorce practice. In mixed membership groups and with consumer audiences, she focuses on her divorce, mediation, and collaborative law practice areas.

Pre-Event Activities

Pre-event activities fall into three categories: research, outreach, and customization of your basic networking tools. The goal is to create, for each meeting, an action plan or "agenda" for maximizing the value of the time you spend participating in the activity—be it a group event or a one-on-one meeting.

Research: Research includes information about the networking organization or event sponsor (if it is new to you), the speakers' backgrounds, and/or group members whom you want to meet. Think about what you want or need to know about the sponsoring entity and its members, and then take a few minutes to Google both speakers and audience members who seem important. Read their biographies, check out their LinkedIn profiles, visit their websites.

If the meeting will spotlight a particular topic you may want to read a relevant article in advance so you can ask intelligent questions. If you unearth a particularly interesting article, you may want to save it to send to people you meet as part of your post-meeting follow-up or to use in one of your LinkedIn group discussions. Research will also help you decide what to emphasize when talking to others.

Outreach: Outreach has two basic centers of attention: people already in your network who will be at the same activity and the attendees you are not connected to yet but would like to meet.

First, think about your contacts and consider who might want to hear these speakers or learn more about the topic. Then connect with them to see if they would like to join you. Second, if no one in your immediate circle is interested, you might put the question to your LinkedIn contacts and see if anyone would like to be your guest.

If an attendance list is available, review it to see whom you want to talk to at the activity. Also annotate the attendance list to get a sense of who will be there. This will help you identify potential referral sources or client prospects who should be on our "to meet" list.

If you are already an active member of the group or organization you might want to connect with someone ahead of time to suggest going to the event together or getting some coffee afterwards. Or if this is a new activity for you, you may want to invite a friend or colleague to go with you to make you feel more comfortable.

When you do go as a group or with another person, be sure to set ground rules about when you will separate and when you will reconnect. If you decide to sit at the same table, leave space between for others to sit in order to maximize your opportunity to meet new people. Also, plan how you can help each other by introducing one another to people you each know who you think might be of interest to the other person.

If the event features a speaker who could help you attain your goals, you could email the person and ask to spend a few minutes with them before or after their speech. The connection becomes more meaningful because you thought of it ahead of time. A lawyer friend who followed this advice, met with a speaker and because of that connection was invited to join their speaker panel at the event the following year.

If there is no speaker, you might want to reach out to others in the organization, for example, their board members or program committee members, and make plans to spend some time together at the event. Again, when you take the time to plan ahead, conversations seem to have more weight than if it is just an ad hoc casual exchange at the event itself.

Agendas: An agenda is a product of your preplanning decisions related to the conversations you want to have and the people you want to network with, and adds a definition of success for the specific activity. An agenda has three segments:

- Topics you want to learn more about by listening to the speaker or asking prepared questions in conversations with other attendees.
- Topics you can discuss as your contribution to conversations. For agenda segments one and two you need to do research. If the meeting topic doesn't lend itself to interesting questions, you can follow Amy Goldsmith's advice to read the newspaper with an eye to developing five questions related to the lead stories.
- How you will measure the success of the activity: This third point of agenda-building is perhaps more important than the other two because it defines the result you want from the meeting and encourages you to measure your activity in terms of the preset results.

An Agenda Example

Activity: Monthly meeting of your general mixed membership networking group with no guests or special topic

1. *Topics I want to learn more about*: the golf tournament the group will host in two months, the background of a new member who might be a good referral source for me
2. *Topics I can discuss as my contribution to conversations*: recent changes in employment law that impact unions [showcases my expertise in labor law], my plans for my summer vacation;
3. *How I will measure the success of the activity*: success will mean:
    - I have sufficient information to decide if I want to participate or sponsor the golf outing;
    - I will meet the new member and if it makes sense will set up a one-on-one follow-up meeting; and
    - I will discuss the new law with a member who is a potential client.

Customization: One key to a successful connection is your ability to reframe your basic tools to match the interests of those who will be at the activity. Begin with creation of your conversation agenda.

- Think first about small talk, those initial pleasantries that precede more robust conversations. Are you most comfortable discussing the weather, the venue, the content of the meeting, sports, something exciting and relevant from the day's news? Have a few observations in mind before you go.
- Or, do you want to ask deeper, more personal or unexpected questions? You can also plan this ahead by considering the kind of people who will be there and then thinking about memorable questions that will intrigue them.
- Or, you can relate your questions to the program topic or issues you know are important to the people you want to meet. For example, you might be going to a meeting about a recently passed law. Questions you could ask others at the meeting include:
    - How long do you think it will take for the state to implement the necessary regulations?
    - How do you think this law will impact your clients?
    - How will you alert your clients to these issues?

As for topics to contribute to your part of the conversation, you could discuss the impact of the new regulations on your clients and how you will alert them to the issue. You could also explain how you plan to turn two provisions of the new law into an opportunity for several of your clients. And you can plan stories to make your discussion more significant to your audience.

"Facts tell, stories sell": Compared to fact-heavy comments, storytelling is a more attention-getting way of explaining what you do. "Research shows that messages delivered as stories can be up to 22 times more memorable than just facts."[2] In Chapter 8, on pages 112–114, we talked about storytelling. Stories resonate because they add context to facts, make us care about the protagonist, and engage our emotions.

> Only one or two minutes may sound too short for a good story, but consider this from a *New York Times* story about the Miss America pageant. 'The candidates were judged on their 20-second answer to two interview questions, eight second descriptions of their social and political platforms, and their 90-second talent performances.'[4]

You can showcase your expertise by highlighting it in the context of a story that is germane to your audience. You can use stories to explain the what and why of your work in a conversational way. Think about the stories you can tell that will reinforce your agenda-points and make your conversation more memorable or "sticky."

Remember stories have three parts:

- The situation
- How it was resolved–what was done
- The result

Stories have a "classic narrative arc. . . . [They] start by establishing the setting and introducing tension through conflict. The turning point, when the tension is at its highest peak is the climax, and what follows is the resolution of the conflict, establishing a new normal for the characters."[3] Typically, your audience cares most about the situation and the result, so go lightly on the specifics of your actions to keep the story to just one to two minutes total.

You want your stories to contribute to your narrative. As part of planning stories, review your basic value proposition and elevator speech and tweak them to make them more meaningful for each audience. You may only need to

2. Sarah Weber, "Does Telling Stories Really Make You 22 Times More Memorable?" https://www.quantifiedcommunications.com/blog/storytelling-22-times-more-memorable.
3. Ibid.
4. "The War for Miss America," *The New York Times*, September 13, 2018, p. D9.

reorder your points or you may want to add something just for one occasion. The best stories invite questions, so think ahead to the kind of questions you want to encourage.

Personal tools for an activity: The final step in preparing for an activity is to put together the tools you will take to the event:

- Your outfit, selected to create the impression you plan to make
- Business cards
- A note pad and pens [one for you and one to share]
- A "cheat sheet" in case you forget some of your preparation or cue up the notes app on your phone

Success: In setting goals for the meeting and defining success, be realistic. For example:

- I want to reconnect with two people and have a meaningful conversation with one new contact.
- I want to learn more about the topic for the meeting so that I can use it to ___________.
- I want to increase my visibility among my target market attendees at the event.

In the post-event stage, you will want to answer the question: Did outcomes from the event itself and your preparations for it move you closer to your goal?

With a goal and an action plan in your back pocket you will have the confidence that preparation brings. If you are an introvert, you will have a research-backed plan to give you a sense of safety and purpose. If you are an extrovert, you will have planned a series of exciting interactions. In both cases, you will have turned a potentially scary, emotional encounter into a planned, productive, rationally designed experience.

At the Event[5]

Look forward to the event and arrive in an interested frame of mind. Arrive early so you can select the seat you want, get a drink before the crush begins, and generally acclimate yourself to the venue. David Abeshouse always prefers to be early, because "you can have some of the best conversations before the crowd arrives."

Focus on quality connections rather than quantity. Networking is not about shaking the most hands and acquiring the most business cards. It is about taking

5. To see event behavior suggestions from the interviewees, please go to Appendix 3, pages 213–215 to read Conversation One-Liners, Conversation Ice Breakers, and Networking Negatives and Corrections.

time to have the conversations that will move a relationship from that first handshake to a trust relationship.

> Karen Haas stresses: 'The most important networking skill is genuine interest in other people. You show interest by asking good, pointed questions, and listening well to the responses.'

Remember your body language so you can maximize your impact in the three seconds when others make their basic assessment of you. Your body language will reflect your attitude.

An interested, upbeat attitude makes other people feel valuable and assures that you are seen in the best possible light. Remember that whenever you meet people you might work with at a later date they will appraise your current interactions as clues to how you would think and act were they to hire you. Intelligent networking conversations will reinforce the perception that you are a smart and knowledgeable professional.

- When you really pay attention to the person you are speaking with and actively listen to them, s/he sees cues to your client service attitude should s/he engage you.
- When you are courteous and polite at networking events it is seen as indicative of your respect for other people and your general approach to interpersonal relations.

To summarize, for the best way to build a meaningful connection with another person, remember these three behaviors:

- "Ask insightful questions (to get the other person thinking). You can know a lot about a person by the quality of the questions he or she asks.
- Ask better questions, receive better answers. . . . By asking better questions when you're speaking with someone, you not only put yourself in a category of someone that thinks differently, but you force the other person to think in a new way that helps him or her grow.
- Pay attention (as if your life depended on it). . . . By simply maintaining eye contact, listening attentively and responding with relevant questions, you're separating yourself from the rest of the pack and are well on your way to fostering a genuine relationship."[6]

---

6. "5 Steps to Seriously Improve Your Networking Skills," May 14, 2015, https://www.entrepreneur.com/article/245995.

Post-Event Activities

A good networking experience is only step one in moving from stranger to trusted friend. If you want a relationship to deepen, you need to interact with the person in a meaningful way eight to ten times during the next 12 months. On a yearly basis this works out to a meaningful "touch" every four to six weeks during the year.

Many of those interviewed see follow-up as the most challenging part of networking.

- How do you find relevant touches after your first follow-up coffee?
- Does putting them on your mailing list and sending them newsletters, alerts, and so on, count as creating touches?
- When moving from meeting to working together takes up to a year, how do you stay top of mind through such a long process?

Some touches can be scheduled as part of your pre-event planning before the next meeting where you will see the person. All follow-up contacts need not be in person. Some can be calls or shared articles related to information of interest to both of you. The point is to be relevant and build on your common interests.

Armanda C. Squadrilli shared a rapport-building story. She sends out periodic postcards about the NYC residential real estate scene, because "the universe will provide but you also need to send out postcards." One of the postcard recipients responded. Before they met, Armanda googled her and learned she raises Hyland cows. When they met in the woman's apartment she saw a picture of the cows on the wall. Her comment was, "I have a cattle dog." Instant rapport.

In your post-meeting connections be careful not to segue from networking attentiveness to sales talk. Nancy Schess, a lawyer and co-founder of Gotham City Networking, shared an example: "It was right after 9/11 and I had just met a banker who called me to let me know that in this time of confusion and upset she was available to open new accounts for people who needed them."

Yet, those I interviewed know they have to schedule follow-up activities because the real relationship-building segment of networking comes in the follow-up and one-on-ones. Amy B. Goldsmith says, "In Vistage one-on-ones happen organically. We see each other at meetings and set up calls or coffee while we are there. Our long-term goal is to get to know these colleagues really well. We know that trust and intimacy only develop over time."

Marcia R. Golden, president of a public relations firm, says, "Meetings hold people accountable for follow-up because you will see those people at the next meeting."

Fred C. Klein says, "When you say you will do something, do it." If you procrastinate, people may equate it with your approach to business deadlines, or they may take your inaction personally and think that you didn't follow-up because you don't like or value them.

Amy B. Goldsmith says, "Successful networking is not rocket science. Do something with forethought. Give because it is important and useful for someone else. If you recognize the seeds planted in conversations centered around helping others, opportunities for business will show themselves."

Categorization: People you meet while networking tend to fall into three "subsequent attention" categories. Think about the criteria you want to use to decide where this person will fit in your networking landscape.

- Category 1: may become a useful connection. Think about linkages with potential relationship people. Anticipate the next two or three touches for each person in this category. Some are people already in your networking universe whom you want to get to know better. Others are newcomers with whom you want to connect to see if the relationship grows into something meaningful.
- Category 2: useful to keep for potential benefit. Add to database in the weak link category; add to your mailing list and perhaps send a LinkedIn request.
- Category 3: not relevant to your goals: Discard. Perhaps nice to know, but not useful in the context of your strategic networking goals.

After an activity, go to your calendar to make notes about the activity itself: Good? Bad? Adequate? Worth doing again? Then turn to your contacts list to update current contacts by adding notes from your conversations, and to add new contacts in category one or two.

After you have added notes to your database and task list, you want to stand back and review the event and your participation in it in order to assess your success in meeting your agenda goals. Were people similar to your target persona at the meeting? Do you need to add to or amend your target persona's personality? Were your stories appropriate and impactful?

Think also about your tools. Did your customization of your elevator speech work well? And your value proposition? Were you able to make it relevant? Did you present your brand image as planned? Reflect on the meeting and ask yourself what you want to do again and what you want to modify.

Note Taking: Sometimes, at the activity, you will be able to jot notes on business cards or in your phone. Sometimes you will have to remember who said what to whom. As soon as possible after any networking encounter, add notes about the conversations you had and the people you met. Add new people to your contacts database and update contacts already on your list with appropriate new information. Pertinent information always includes the meeting location, date (including the year), and topics discussed. Don't limit your notes to business talk. Add personal information that comes up in conversation, such as birthdays, trips, and other key events in their lives. You may even want to send a baby present, or the names of some restaurants from a location you have visited that they plan to visit. Again, the cost is not as important as the thought behind the gift.

It may seem like a waste of time to note all the details, but if you do you will be able to refresh your memory more completely before the next encounter. Good note-taking enables you to begin the next conversation where you left off.

Connecting Options–Mail: Group meetings are important access points to get to know a variety of people who will become either weak or strong relationships. Timing is important when reaching out. Follow-ups need to happen as soon as possible. You want to reference the shared experience while the memory of it and of you is still warm.

Contacts in the potential relationship category should receive an email follow-up, a snail mail note, or a phone call. If you reached out to people during your pre-event activities and they did not come to the meeting or you were unable to connect with them at the meeting, send a follow-up email or call to say you were sorry to miss them. For those who were absent, add a line or two highlighting what they missed.

> "Jessica Thaler-Parker, an attorney working in regulatory change and project management in NYC, says, 'Follow-up and follow-through are essential. You need to be prompt to show your respect for the other person's time.'"

Follow-up emails and letters are most successful when they are personalized. Instead of saying, "I enjoyed meeting you," it is more effective to say "I enjoyed comparing notes with you about __________." Or "I will take your advice and __________." Or "I will research ________ and get back to you." This moves the note from routine to personal and from information to information with an emotional connection. If you can, add value by introducing the other person to someone s/he might like to know or send him/her material that relates back to your discussion.

Connecting Options–In person: For category one people you will want to build the relationship initially through one-on-one encounters; anything from quick cups of coffee to lunch or social events. It is in one-on-ones that you can really learn about the other person's priorities, motivations, work ethic, approach to clients, family relationships, hobbies, etc. Trust and shared work initiatives build upon in-depth relationships.

> "Marcia Golden says she can 'feel shy' in group settings, so she appreciates the rules that force her to be social. 'It is easier to make connections and suggest one-on-one follow-ups because [in groups] it is expected.'"

At each networking event you might identify one or two people you want to really get to know better in the next six months. They could be relevant to your goals for a variety of reasons:

- You share the same target market.
- You work with or have worked with the same client.
- There are synergies between their practice and yours.
- They are interested in referring you or you are interested in referring them.
- They add resources.
- They are good company–fun to be around.

For these few people, plot out a connections diagram showing where and how your lives overlap, the commonalities you share, and the ways in which you can help each other. In your post-event written note, add a follow-up action step. Activities could include:

- Arranging another meeting just one-on-one or inviting others you think the person might find of interest
- Introducing them to people who might help them attain their goals
- Finding resources for them
- Sending them materials that relate to the conversation you had

In the world before mobile phones, the difference between emails and handwritten notes was relatively unimportant. Today when US mail is mostly a vehicle for bills and catalogues, finding a piece of really personal mail becomes an event.

Two examples of follow-up gone right and gone wrong. Nancy Schess, a lawyer and co-founder of Gotham City Networking, shared the following story of attentiveness gone wrong.

"A week after my Dad died, I received a condolence card that appropriately expressed sympathy but then spoiled it by saying, 'Let me know when you want to do a meet and greet.'"

Personal notes done right can reinforce the impact of the impression you made in person. For example, Stacy Francis, a financial planner, sends a handwritten, personal note after every one-on-one meeting. She minimizes the time it takes by assigning a staff member to address the envelope and draft the notes based on her meeting logs. Then, every Friday, she sits with the week's batch of note cards and writes them up quickly. If you like this idea, be sure to buy high quality, personalized note cards.

Chapter Summary

Strategic networking in practice moves from the why of selecting the activity to preparation for best behavior at the event to follow-up to solidify connections. An assessment of the preparation, actions, and follow-up allows you to fine-tune your strategic plans as you move forward. Mastering networking techniques helps you analyze networking opportunities, chose the best ones for you, and then learn the techniques that will showcase your value to others.

In the next chapter we look at a special, important category of relationships–referrals.

The Art of Giving and Getting Referrals 11

Referrals Are Part-Art, Part-Strategy

Referrals are sometimes called networking gold. In strategic networking, referrals are an end product of a plan focused on meeting specific people who are able to introduce you to potential clients and relevant sources. The purpose of referral-focused strategies is to identify and meet those people who can help you reach your goals.

The process of making referrals is partly art because it requires sensitive balancing to put people together and the best referrers seem to have a sixth sense about connections and timing. Of course, for referrers, making introductions is also a strategy in that the referrer needs to decide which requests to fill, whom to ask to take a referral, and so on.

> "Referrals are an end product of a plan focused on meeting specific people who are able to introduce you to potential clients and relevant sources."

Anyone can be a referrer. Good referrers hear the need for introductions in ordinary conversation. For example, a young mother talks about being worried about going back to work. A good listener will broaden the conversation to ask if the woman needs a nanny or a referral to a day care center. Or, an accountant says he is looking for more restaurant clients. The good listener may probe to find out what kind of restaurants and then be able to offer introductions.

Effective referrers usually have large heterogenous networks, resource-rich due to a wide variety of weak and strong links. If your network is reasonably large and diverse it increases the likelihood that someone you know may be helpful to someone else.

- Often, people ask for introductions to personal service people who may have nothing to do with your day job but may be in your network because you know them.
- Or, they are going to a conference in another city where you have contacts you can suggest they meet.
- Or, professionals interested in a new subject may ask a weak link in their own network to introduce them to people they know who can help them.

> "Larry Hutcher, co-managing partner of a midsize firm and a master referrer, says, 'Good networkers are givers. Give first because it always comes back to you. I always ask, "How can I help you?" Later I explain what my firm does and follow by saying, "I'd love to represent you."'"

The key to successful referral requests is specificity. If you ask to meet anyone who might need someone who does what you do, the possibilities seem infinite. Too vague a request is difficult for the referrer to remember. If you make the request very specific—I'd like to meet the in-house lawyer for the teamsters union—it is easier for referrers to help you reach the specific person.

In addition to helping a networker implement his/her plan, the process of referring makes people feel good. Emotionally, as a species, we are hardwired to collaborate. We want to help other people in our group, our tribe, our network. Helping others and being helped by them adds an emotional component to strategic requests. When someone accepts a referral request both people feel good.

Two colleagues include referral statements at the end of their emails that connect the "who" to the "why" of referral-focused networking.

A travel agent in one of my networking groups says, "A referral is sending someone you care about to someone you trust."[1]

Similarly, Stacy Francis' emails say: "Referrals from our clients and trusted professionals are a great compliment and one of the benchmarks by which we measure our success in meeting clients' needs. We thank you for your

---

1. Laura Avital, member of Gotham Networking Group, Long Island Women's Chapter.

continuous support and hope you will pass along our information to anyone you feel would benefit from our services."[2]

Your referral needs are usually related to client-focused goals. Look back at the planning work you did in Chapters 2 and 8 and identify the specific prospects you want to meet. Review your strategy for connecting with people who can and will introduce you to those potential clients.

Viewed as a strategic networking asset, referrals take their rightful place as a major resource to be cared for, protected, and encouraged. Many interviewees offered insights into how they do this.

Lenny Carraturo, Wells Fargo middle market banking business development officer, tells a story that illustrates the importance of an intentional referral strategy, in this case helped by a bit of serendipity. Len networks primarily with accountants, lawyers, and financial executives. In this example, a CPA colleague called regarding a client who wanted a construction loan in order to build a new office. While Len was preparing a description of three loan products for the person to consider, a lawyer, another part of his strategic network, called him for help related to the acquisition of the building—for the same client. Len was able to facilitate both deals and satisfy his two referral sources and the client.

Andrew C. Peskoe, head of his firm's corporate practice group, says that he grew one of his industry practices through serendipity, but the anecdote also reflects his broad contact base.

- First, a key service provider for people in the industry was referred to him by an existing client.
- Then, a friend turned out to also be a leading provider to that same industry.
- Then, he helped a family member's friend who turned out to be a major player in the same industry.
- These three industry referrers helped Andy grow this industry practice exponentially.

For Andy you might say that connections + karma = business.

In this chapter we will look at four personal aspects of referral practice:

- Referral definitions: referrer, connector, referred, and referred-to
- Referral strategies

2. Email from Stacy Francis.

- Referral etiquette
- Referral tracking

Definition of Players

In any referral there are at least three players:

- *Referrer*: the person who makes an introduction
- *Referred*: the person who asks the referrer for a referral, the person the referrer is going to introduce
- *Referred-to*: an awkward term for the person the referrer thinks will fulfill a need that is sometimes voiced by the referred and, other times, identified by the referrer

Referral relationships move between the three actors in reciprocal ways.[3] For example,

- A lawyer who wants an introduction [*referred*] asks a colleague [*referrer*] to introduce him to an insurance agent [*referred-to person*].
- The following week, the *referred-to* insurance agent asks the *referred* lawyer to introduce him to other lawyers in his firm's employment practice. The *referred* in step one now becomes a *referrer*.
- A month later, the insurance agent, having already participated as referred-to and referred, becomes the *referrer* when he invites the first referrer [who asked him to meet the lawyer] to meet a client of his.

Connectors: My definition of connectors reflects my conclusion about these kinds of networkers based on my interviews with many of them and my own networking experiences over the last 25 years. My definition is straightforward: Connectors are known for the linkages they create among people. Connectors are networkers known for the quality of their networks and their willingness to share that network to help others. Their strategy entails judicious use of their network to both help others and enhance their own sphere of influence.

Connectors are usually the most popular individuals at any networking event. They seem to have a personal magnetism that attracts others. They are always "on," always interested in what others are saying, always focused on whomever they are talking to, always actively listening. Connectors are approachable matchmakers, generous with their time.

You can recognize a connector mentality in conversations because they are always offering resources.

- How can I help you?

---

3. Most professions have ethics rules that inhibit various aspects of networking, especially in the area of referrals. Be sure you know the rules of your profession before you set your strategy.

- I think I know someone who could use your services, *or* could help you, *or* you could help.
- Do you know Charlie Brown? I think he would be very interested in what you do. *Or* I think he had a situation similar to yours. *Or* I think you both have a lot in common.

Connectors' personal connection grids are both wide and deep. An extensive network of weak relationships with people offering a comprehensive variety of skills and occupations balances the tight circle of people with whom they have deep, strong relationships. Into this world come people who want or need introductions to the people in their networks.

Connectors broker requests for resources, such as nannies, nurses, financial planners, lawyers, dentists, baseball tickets, restaurant reservations, and everything in-between, be it professional or personal. Of course, many requests are for introductions that will help the referred to build his/her own business.

Connectors usually don't need to ask directly for business leads for themselves. Their seat at the hub of interlocking networks promotes their own brand. Their place in the networking system keeps them top of mind among their connections when relevant business opportunities arise.

Why do connectors make these introductions?

- Their minds naturally go to connections when someone requests a favor. As a friend of mine explained, "I make referrals because my mind makes automatic connections. My internal Rolodex flips open when someone asks me about referrals."
- Connecting people makes them feel good because they can help others. They practice the "give to get" mantra.
- They use referrals to grow their own network strategically and keep themselves visible within it.
- Finally, they acknowledge the personal power inherent in the connector role that reinforces their trusted advisor status with clients, colleagues, friends, and friends of friends.

If there is a networker's hierarchy, rainmakers are at the top. Among rainmakers, connectors are rainmakers who continually bring in business as a corollary of their referral activities. "Rainmakers know that the issue isn't finding people who might refer business, but rather, developing relationships with the handful of people who can help you get the kind of business you want."[4] Rainmaker-connectors want to create beneficial connections—referrals that advance the goals of all parties.

---

4. Carol Greenwald and Laura Wexler, "Keeping Alive the Golden Goose of Referrals," *Strategies: The Journal of Legal Marketing*, July 2006, pp. 4–7.

Referral Strategies

Ask most successful professionals where their new business comes from and they usually say from referrals. Where do these referrals come from? The typical answer is "anywhere and everywhere." Certainly, coincidence and chance lead to some referrals. Perhaps from your best client, your best friend or a stranger who sits next to you on a plane. Unplanned referrals can happen as a result of good work or being in the right place at the right time or knowing the right person.

Strategic networking offers more control because referrals are frequently a strategy to implement your plan to secure your growth goals. These strategies are built around and out of relationships you develop within your network, and through links with your contacts' networks. Think broadly when considering where to look for referrers. Potential categories include:

- Work-related connections
  - Current or past co-workers in your firm or business
  - People who serve the same target market
  - Other professionals who work with your clients
  - People in complementary fields whose clients need your services
  - Professionals who cannot or do not want to handle a situation
  - Clients past and present
- Online connections
  - People who know you or who you know of you through your outreach activities in various online venues
  - Online listservs and groups where your colleagues or target market converse
- Friends and family, including:
  - College alumni, mentors, teachers
  - Family members and their connections
  - People you know in your community, church, synagogue, club
  - Members of your nonprofit boards or committees

Introductions serve many purposes. They can:

- Provide career-related opportunities and advice
- Lead to new business opportunities
- Offer openings for marketing and increased visibility
- Give rise to idea exchanges presenting new insights and information
- Grow your practice in an efficient, effective, targeted way
- Make it easier to move more quickly to a comfort level in a new relationship when you can reference the referrer's credibility
- Add to referrers' "social currency"
- Add resources that will be useful to you and/or your clients
- Introduce you to people who service the same target market
- Lead to new friendships

Building a Referrals Program: When you begin to build a referrals program think broadly about the kinds of groups and individuals who come in contact with or have access to your desired targets. A solid referrer strategy is built on a foundation of strong relationships with people who understand what you do and are willing to help you move toward your goals.

Networks anchored by strong links that also include a wide variety of weak links often offer the best opportunities for introductions because they balance those who know you well with those who are well-connected in areas you don't know.

To create a supportive referral network, you should first revisit the depiction of your target persona, in Chapter 8, and your SWOT analysis, in Chapter 2. Remind yourself of your target niche as you look to develop referral relationships. Then turn to Worksheet 11.1 Referral Strategies Worksheet [Appendix 2, pages 203–205] to help you integrate your referral goals with your other strategic networking priorities.

Where should you begin? Begin with clients who rave about you. Make sure family, friends, co-workers and neighbors know what you do so that when asked, "Do you know a good [fill in the blank]?" they can suggest you.

Look for people in complementary fields who are interested in the same target market and suggest creating a collaborative referral strategy. Begin with professional colleagues who share clients with you or who pursue the same industries or demographic groups.

- If you do mergers and acquisitions you might look for referrers among your professional colleagues—lawyers, accountants, bankers, brokers, venture capitalists. You might join a group such as Vistage where you could meet CEOs, business leaders, as well as professionals in complementary services.
- If you work with the elderly, potential referrers could include all the professionals just mentioned plus doctors, family members, medical personnel, operators of senior citizen homes and long-term care facilities, insurance brokers, wealth managers, social workers, and religious leaders. You could join a variety of groups from trade associations to AARP.

Colleagues in your own profession should not be overlooked. Think about people you worked with in previous positions or your mentors or professionals in firms that charge more than you do. All these people could be referral resources when they are conflicted out of doing the work or don't want to take the client. Usually it is easier to get work from colleagues if you have a narrow niche practice or work in a boutique firm because there is less opportunity for conflict.

No referral strategy is perfect for all time. It must change as your goals change. You should examine your key relationships annually to see where your universe is sufficiently robust and where you need to add breadth or depth. Determine what is missing, what connections are no longer relevant, and which areas need expansion.

Making a Referral: Favors rarely involve a quid pro quo arrangement; but, the intent, often unspoken, is to try to help those who help you. And so, favors go 'round and 'round—an ever-flowing personal currency that gives substance to the Gotham City Networking Group networking mantra "what goes around, comes around."

The actual practice of giving and receiving referrals is an informal system of favors requested and fulfilled.

- When a referrer asks someone else [the referred-to] to share time, information, access, or work with someone [the referred], they are using up a favor with the someone else because they are asking that individual to do something for someone because the referrer asked them to.
- The referred, that is, the person who gains access to the referred-to person, uses up a favor with the referrer and owes a return favor down the road.
- The person referred-to gains favors with the referrer if s/he meets with the referred, even if the introduction leads nowhere.

Not all referrals are of equal quality. As Figure 11.1 shows, referrals can be grouped into the following five categories:

- *Best*: The referrer makes a personal introduction and offers to be involved in the introductory phase. Sometimes you all meet together for coffee or a meal; other times the referrer offers some other form of personal involvement.
- *Good*: The referrer makes a call to the referred-to individual and then reports back to the referred with an answer. If it is a go, the referred takes the next step alone.
- *Adequate*: Email introductions where the referrer sends an email to both people, with contact information and an explanation indicating the basis for the introduction and suggests they take it from there.
- *Poor*: Email introductions that only give contact information after a throw-away line such as "I thought it would be useful for you two to meet"—the equivalent of a blind date.
- *Useless*: "Call so-and-so." Name dropping without any accompanying contact information or reasons for offering the names is useless, as is recommending that the referred say, "Charlie suggested I call you."

Done well the role of referrer is time-consuming because it requires thinking about relevant introductions, making them, and then following through to ensure that a productive connection happens.

Figure 11.1 Continuum of Referrals

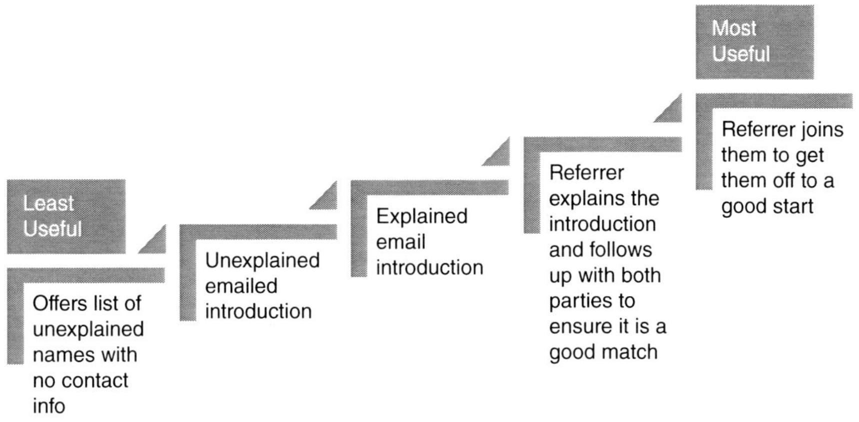

Several people interviewed shared examples of the kind of referral activity they prefer:

Marcia R. Golden, president of DJD Golden, spends the time necessary to make what she calls "intelligent referrals." Before she makes introductions, she calls the referred-to person to get their permission to make the introduction. Then she'll send an email introduction to both people and offer to "quarterback their meeting" to promote success. Quarterbacking means that she might go to the first meeting with them or call the referred-to person to reinforce her reasons for the introduction. She expects to find out the next time they see each other at a group meeting if the referral worked out.

Jeffrey A. Blutstein, a financial planner, says he is "a good feeder of business to others because it is important to give leads." When he makes a referral, he often begins the conversation by saying, "I'm imposing on our good relationship and asking you to meet X 'and the reason I am imposing on your 'good offices' is I know you and I know Ms. X. It will be to your mutual benefit to meet.' It is important for me to couch this as a favor to me. THAT should be the only reason my referrals see each other."

Martin S. Klein, a trust and estates lawyer, considers connectors the best networkers because they remember who needs what, and when opportunities arise generate introductions. When Marty refers he follows up after the introduction to make sure the connection happens.

The referral process requires collaborations built on trust. Trust is the essential precondition, because to refer involves an element of risk.

- If you are helping someone else obtain work, you are taking yourself out of an equation in which you have promised A that B has the appropriate expertise, experience, and client service attitude to resolve A's problems in the way A likes them resolved. You are trusting that B will make good on your promise.
- If you are helping someone with a job search you are directly asking the referred-to to advise the referred, and implicitly asking them to offer introductions as well.
- If you are offering resources you are assuming the referred-to will do good work for the referred.

Sometimes something goes wrong. B may put A's client on the back burner, or do a poor job, or backstab A and steal the client. You vouched for B, so if the relationship between A and B sours, you stand to lose a friend, a colleague, and most importantly, some of your social capital. If you offer a connection as an information resource and they share nothing of value, you as the referrer may lose face with the referred. Similarly, if you share resources.

Some behaviors can sever referral relationships. In a survey of law firm referral sources, Sally Schmidt found four personality factors that annoyed non-attorney referrers when they referred lawyers because they adversely impact service quality:

- Two aspects of unresponsiveness—slow response or unreturned telephone calls
- Two aspects of "lawyering" —arrogance and overcomplicating a matter[5]

Ordinarily, the blame for any snafu falls back onto the referrer; so referrals are not offered lightly. Ronald K. Stair, an actuary and principal of a retirement plan design firm, hosts weekly invitation-only small luncheons. He only invites "people who are referable" because that means he can make introductions and never worry about them. Ron believes that making referrals is serious business, because "when someone is referred, they are lent the referrer's credibility."

One consultant suggests that the following qualities make a person referable:

- Trust. Do you live up to your promises and claims?
- Value. Do you demonstrably improve the client's condition?
- Responsiveness. Are you accessible, and do you respond rapidly?
- Credibility. Does the client feel it's impressive to be partnering with you?
- Reciprocity. Do you recommend people to the client where appropriate?

---

5. Sally J. Schmidt, "Developing New Business by Developing Relationships," The Practical Lawyer, ALI-ABA, June 1999.

- Professionalism. Are you on time and on deadline?
- Innovation. Are you leading edge? State of the art?
- Reputation. Are you seen by others as being the best of the best?"[6]

Successful networkers don't boast about these qualities. Rather, they demonstrate them in everyday interactions with everyone they meet.

Sidebar 11.1 Examples of Thoughtful Referrals

Referrals among individuals focused on the same market:

- *A public relations professional introduces two clients: the manager of a famous NYC building and a construction firm CEO.*
- *A coach introduced two clients: one who needs organizational skills and the other a professional organizer.*
- *A consultant introduces two lawyers in complementary fields.*

Referrals when need complementary expertise:

- *A corporate attorney refers a technology client to a patent firm.*
- *A management-side employment attorney offers the name of an employee-side employment law firm to their client so that the person bringing the suit has solid representation.*
- *A banker refers a client to a lawyer and an accountant.*

Resources referrals:

- *A financial planner offers clients the names of divorce attorneys, trust and estate attorneys, employment attorneys, insurance brokers, realtors, nanny agencies, as needed.*
- *A divorce lawyer introduces realtors, trust and estate lawyers, and child psychologists to clients.*
- *A real estate professional shares names of day care centers, preschools, insurance brokers, contractors, and electricians.*

Referral Networking Examples: Many people join groups to find appropriate referrers. Often young professionals or those new to a profession remain active in school groups in order to continue relationships with academic and internship mentors for career-related introductions and advice.

Workplace alumni groups become important referral sources for professionals who want to share clients when a referrer is unable or uninterested in doing

6. Alan Weiss, Million Dollar Referrals, quoted in "How to Become Super-Referable?" hubspot.com, January 23, 2015.

work for the client. For example, James K. Landau, partner at McCarthy Fingar, met an attorney at a firm alumni event. She subsequently invited him to visit her networking group. At one of her group's meetings he got to know another lawyer who introduced him to a prospect who became a client.

On his website, David Abeshouse, who focuses on B2B dispute resolution, describes the where and why of his referral strategy, which is the cornerstone of his practice-building strategy. "I regularly serve on the boards of New York not-for-profit corporations and help to run several legal and business networking groups, enabling me to develop and foster a broad and deep network of trusted professionals on whom I can rely to assist my clients and colleagues for matters that are outside the areas of my expertise."

His website also comments on the role referrals play in his practice's growth: "My law practice is not built on advertising, rather it is founded upon referrals—referrals from valued clients, trusted professional colleagues and friends, and others who have benefitted from working or affiliating with me."

Bar association luncheon networking groups present similar opportunities to get to know people in other firms, in other practice areas or focused on similar target markets, all of whom are potential referral sources. Often vendors who market to lawyers belong to these groups. Lawyers look to these vendors for resources and clients.

People focused on the same market regularly network not only with those in that market but also with those who service the same market. Often, they piggyback their services. Other times, they draw from their contacts pool to make introductions for colleagues. Collaberex is an example of a group explicitly built on this model. Associations of law firms, such as Primerus, incorporate the expectation of referrals among member firms.

In-person, general membership networking groups normally have a "leads wanted" section of the meeting where people ask who knows someone in *x* company or *y* position or they ask for introductions to specific decision makers. Some single profession groups, such as The Attorney Roundtable and The International Network of Boutique & Independent Law Firms were founded to provide a set of trusted, vetted professionals for the purpose of referrals. Ellen Volpe's ABA group members fill out a personal referral roadmap identifying names of referral sources [who can refer the person to their contacts] and referral partners [to whom the ABA member can refer].[7]

7. Shared at a meeting Greenwald attended, October 12, 2017.

Richard Friedman, a management side employment litigator for management, has built his firm on referrals from former colleagues in the big law firms he previously worked in plus other lawyers and professionals in related fields whom he meets in networking groups. He actively participates in four or five lawyer-only or general membership networking groups. In professional associations he usually holds leadership positions, which increases his visibility and contacts pool. When he meets someone at these meetings that he feels is a good referral resource, he suggests a one-on-one meeting. Sometimes, he has several such meetings in a day. He is a connector who not only wants referrals but makes them. As he says, "I follow up with people for our mutual benefit."

Some professionals look for referral relationships in the professional or trade associations of their target market. They attend meetings and seek other opportunities within the group's structure to write or speak in order to showcase their expertise and heighten their visibility.

Community-based organizations offer focused opportunities to give back and at the same time meet other like-minded people. Board members meet people who enhance the quality of their lives and when it is possible, hire them. Steve Smith, an accountant and a member of several arts-related boards, recommends the experience both "for the chance to expand your store of knowledge and, over time as relationships mature, obtain business."

Referrer Education: When you want to ask someone for a favor—a referral—you need to do most of the work in terms of clarifying what you want, why you want it, and how it will help you. Don't expect the referrer to do your thinking for you. Nobody knows "anybody" or "everybody," so vague requests rarely pan out.

A vague request—"I'd like to meet lawyers who want to increase their business" or bankers or wealth managers—is really an imposition because it presupposes that the referrer will have the time and knowledge to figure out what would be satisfactory for you. Instead, "Attorneys need to create a referral strategy that includes a systematic approach to educating referral sources what a good referral looks like and how to make it."[8]

The person seeking a referral should make the ask easier by explaining to the referrer exactly what s/he is looking for, including why s/he is making the request. Think back to your target market and craft a specific description of what

8. Stephen Fairley, "3 Myths and 5 Truths Every Attorney Should Know About Referrals," June 2018, http://plaintiffattorneymarketing.com/3-myths-and-5-truths-every-attorney-should-know-about-referrals/

you are looking for. Identify the relevant characteristics of your niche and the benefits those clients obtain from your work. Share:

- Factual details about your practice and the key characteristics of the clients you want
- Stories that illustrate the kind of problems you solve
- Trigger words to listen for that suggest a need for your expertise
- Language for the referrer to use when describing your services

It is important to pay attention to your words with a focus on open-ended questions that do not prejudge an answer or create unnecessary dead ends.

A lawyer with an ADA disabilities practice sets up a meeting with a social worker in the Department of Social Services. She explains in detail who she works with, why she does it, and how her cases play out [using stories that highlight the emotional tensions involved and downplaying the jargon]. Then the lawyer asks the social worker how best to meet potential clients.

How she asks questions will influence the conversation and the answers. If she asks a yes/no question, "Can you introduce me to the person in charge of nursing homes?" she has created a possible conversation dead end. Whether the social worker says "yes" and makes the introduction, or "no" and shuts down, the effect is to close off the chance to learn about opportunities. If she asks an open-ended question such as, "Where do you think people with my skill set can be most useful?" the conversation can continue along any number of helpful tracks.

The more concrete you can make a request the more likely you are to find referrers who will help you. Figure 11.2 provides an example of a useful drill down. You begin looking at baby boomers and then focus on those who have recently retired because they should need your services to remortgage their home, revise their will, and so forth.

As you increase the specificity of your referral requests, you will also increase the volume of useful introductions. Specificity makes it easier for others to think of you when your key situations arise. Here are a few more examples:

- Begin by identifying a broad industry or demographic category: shipping or restaurants, baby boomers, entrepreneurs, elderly couples.
- Then drill down to a subgroup such as retiring baby boomers, tech entrepreneurs, divorcing elderly couples. Or pick American shipping companies that move freight, national chains of grocery stores, or fast food restaurants.
- Drill down farther still to say what specific issues or problems you want to focus on.

Figure 11.2 Drilling Down from a Broad Group to a Specific Niche

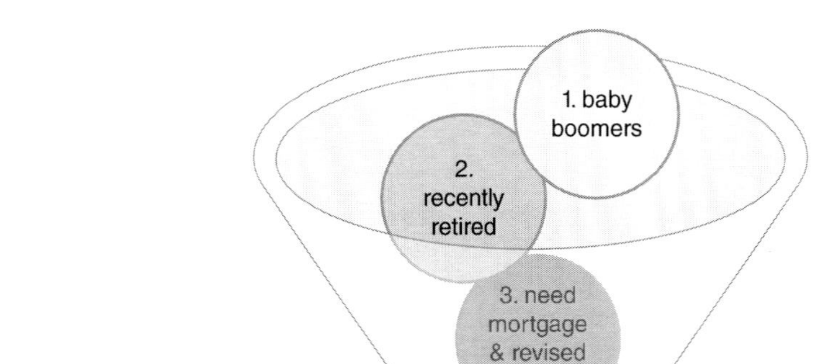

Referral conversations set expectations for both sides. They help you find what you are looking for on the presumption that you will reciprocate. Make sure to ask your referrer what s/he is looking for. Even if you are not in the habit of making referrals, opportunities often arise. If you know what the referrer wants, you can be alert to openings for them.

Sometimes the reverse happens: You help someone who never reciprocates. Assume they never thought of it, and next time you help them add: "Let me tell you what I am working on so that you can listen in your network for people who could use my services. I would appreciate it."

> "David Rosenbaum, an IT professional says he is only looking for 'Oh s___t!' situations where his company can come in and save the client. These become his best clients because in the process of rescuing them he creates a relationship that leads to continued business."

Referral Etiquette

No matter the source of a referral, all participants need to mind their manners. Many potential relationships are sabotaged by poor communication among the referrer, the referred, and the referred-to. To prevent miscommunication, remember two key words: feedback and courtesy.

Feedback Loops: Feedback keeps connections alive. It provides a chance to monitor how the referred relationship is working out. It keeps the referrer in the loop so that should s/he run into the referred-to person s/he will be able to say something appropriate. Referrers dislike being blindsided when the referred-to person alludes to interactions they don't know about.

The Referrer: If the referrer is courteous, s/he will:

- Tell the referred if and when they can use his/her name.
- Call the referred-to to find out if s/he agrees that the referral is appropriate and ask permission before giving his/her name to the person seeking the referral.
- Participate in the introduction.
- Follow-up with the referred-to person in two weeks to make sure everything is going smoothly.
- At the end of the engagement, reconnect with both parties to find out how it went. Thank the referred-to.

The Referred: Once a referral is in play, it is only polite for the referred to contact the referrer at key points.

- Thank the referrer for the introduction.
- Follow up promptly and let the referrer know what happened.
  - If a meeting occurs, let the referrer know it happened, and perhaps your assessment of the meeting.
  - If you are hired, let the referrer know at the beginning of the engagement and when it ends.
  - If the connection fails, let the referrer know and perhaps explain why you think it didn't work out.
- Always thank everybody—every time.

The Referred-To: The referred-to also has etiquette to follow:

- If s/he does not want the referral, s/he should tell the referrer why, so the referrer doesn't make this error again.
- Once the referred and referred-to meet, the latter should again touch base with the referrer so everyone is on the same page.
- At the conclusion of the shared experience, the referred-to should share his/her evaluation of the experience with the referrer as a way of improving the process.

This kind of etiquette not only keeps everyone involved up to date on what's happening; more importantly, it provides educational feedback that increases the value of the referral.

Referral Tracking

Referral relationships need to be well managed so that you know who has helped you, how much the help meant to you, and how you have been able to repay the favors. If you rely on memory, you tend to focus on the most immediate encounter, forgetting key people who were perhaps more useful several months ago.

Tracking creates a valuable memory assist. Monthly reports highlight where relationships are producing quality introductions and collaborations, and where the process is misdirected. You can then make a strategic decision to focus on reinforcing the current quality relationships or decide to widen or reorganize your referral base.[9]

> "As Roger Barton, managing partner of Barton LLP says: 'There are only so many referrals to give out. So, it is important to keep track of them and work with others who understand the value of an interconnected relationship.'"

Chapter Summary

The hallmark of an effective referral strategy is a strong referral network composed of carefully chosen people you like and trust, who like and trust you, share common interests, and collaborate to help each other find the resources and develop the business each one wants.

9. For a sample of a referral database, see Carol Greenwald and Laura Wexler, "Keeping Alive the Golden Goose of Referrals," *Strategies: The Journal of Legal Marketing*, July 2006; Greenwald and Wexler, "Turning Referrals Into Gold," *New York Law Journal*, Solos and Small Firms Supplement, June 26, 2006.

Putting It All Together: Integrating, Evaluating, and Measuring Activities 12

Measurement should be the final segment of an unfolding plan. Once you have developed and played out a strategy it would seem prudent to examine it in order to improve the next iteration. I naively thought all the expert networkers I interviewed would have complex evaluation and measurement systems. Turns out I thought wrong.

Two-thirds of them don't quantitatively measure the outcomes of their activities. They think qualitatively, in broad strokes:

- "Am I enjoying it?"
- "How am I doing in terms of friendships, visibility, and other qualitative measures?"
- "Metrics aren't necessary. I am small enough to know."
- "My metrics are my expenses on my tax return."
- "I track marketing hours—I see the results."

Those who do any tracking tend to focus on contacts, jotting notes after meetings, adding names to a tickler file, or tracking referral interactions. Only two people among the interviewees, both in firms with CRM systems, use them to focus on key metrics such as ROI, time in the leads pipeline, and personal time.

A handful of interviewees offered personal tracking or evaluation examples:

James K. Landau, a lawyer, spends the first half hour of every day reviewing his contact management systems lists, key names, and so on. He tracks activities in Outlook folders and subfolders and reviews them to determine where to expend his efforts.

Stacey Cohen, president of a PR agency, uses the LinkedIn ROI social selling index to measure engagement success.

Lenny Carraturo, commercial business development officer at Wells Fargo Bank, tracks his interactions on an Excel spreadsheet noting those he meets with and those with whom he exchanges leads.

Andrew C. Peskoe, a lawyer, keeps his own calendar, and schedules client or networking lunches almost every day.

The interviewees' answers about tracking reflect real life, especially among a group of self-assured, effective practitioners of the art of strategic networking. But as you begin to practice strategic networking it is useful to review some evaluation and measurement best practices. We will also consider some ideas for turning strategic networking into a habit that you practice regularly.

Plan Management

Your plan is a living, breathing entity that changes as the environment and your goals change. So, every month you should:

- Review your calendar for the coming month to make sure the activities will have a cumulative impact—moving you toward your goals.
- Set your task list with due dates and reminder times to ensure that your networking tasks are accomplished on schedule.
- Remember strategic networking is an investment in your future. Make yourself as accountable for these activities as you are for your billable time.

Also track networking time and dollars for reimbursement purposes and as necessary data for quarterly success evaluations.

Time categories include time spent on the following activities:

- Marketing plan development and assessments of what is and is not working, what to tweak, what to drop and what to rev up.
- Evaluation and updating of target niches, target markets, client personas, and strategic networking goals.
- Assessment of the effectiveness of your elevator speech and experience stories to fine-tune what you want to share about the value of your skill set and experience.
- Updates to your contacts database coded by industry, resource usefulness, interactions, and so on. Remember to include personal details like

children's birthdays and also when and how you met, why you connected, and conversation highlights.
- Time capture of both group and one-on-one meetings, including the time spent on the pre- and post-event activities: setting up the meeting, research in preparation for your meeting agenda, the meeting itself, and the time to complete your follow-up activities.
- Preparation time for articles, speeches, blogs, and so forth.
- Marketing activities planned and shared with people in your firm, colleagues in complementary service areas, and others among your contacts.
- Training classes in marketing and business development.

After you analyze your strategy, adjust your goals and your networking activities related to those goals. Use Worksheet 12.1 Networking Evaluation Report [Appendix 2, page 206] to capture your analysis.

- Decide if you want to increase participation in successful activities.
- Analyze why some plans are not working as you anticipated.
- Then tweak the laggards and try again.
- Be sure you continue to network in niches and focus on changes in your target markets.

Organization Involvement Assessments

You should track activities and results related to each organization you join. Begin with why you joined and what you expected. Then document your efforts to become part of the group—working on committees, joining the leadership, and so on. Track the people you've met, what you've done together, and successes stemming from each group. Reviewing the qualitative and quantitative data will suggest whether to continue on with your plan, amend it, or leave current organizations to try some other networking locales.

> "Marcia R. Golden, president of a public relations agency, says, 'Organizations have a shelf life. You need to stay a minimum of a year, and usually about year three move on to other groups. Sometimes people overstay their time in a group ether because they value the people and friendships or because they fail to notice the fall off in productiveness.'"

The interviewees agreed that most people remain in groups related to their strategic goals for three to five years. By then they have probably exhausted the opportunities in the group. They usually maintain their close relationships with some members of the group. As their business development efforts produce results, they refine their networking strategies. They move to more targeted entities such as industry groups, niche membership groups, or create their own private groups.

Referral Tracking

As noted in Chapter 11, measuring the quality of referral-focused interactions can help you identify those with whom the interplay is most advantageous. Whether you use a computer program, Excel spreadsheet, or paper and pencil, you should track the following aspects:

- Obviously, the name, contact information, and industry of the individual
- How you met the person
- The quantity and quality of referrals in and out
  - To whom, from whom, with whom
    - Be sure to note if you are the referrer, referred, or referred-to
  - Purpose of the referral:
    - Business
    - Personal
    - Resources
    - Fun
  - Appropriateness of the referral
  - Quality of your interactions with the referrer and those to whom you are referred
  - The value to you of the referral
    - Monetary value
    - Intangible values, such as friendship, reputation enhancement, and so on
- Other rewards from relationship, for example, shared visibility opportunities, introductions to key resources, and the like

The headings on your tracking sheet should reflect whatever is important to you about these resources, for example, their expertise, industry, the target market you share with them, the depth of the relationship, and so on. When more than one person in your firm or close circle of contacts knows the same referrer, you should note that as well, either to work together or to stay out of each other's way.

You can also correlate referral activities with your prospecting activities in terms of people you've met, cultivated, and begun to work with, or resources you were able to offer others in your network. You might want to track the impact of your referral relationships on:

- The quality of your network
- The role of referrers in the growth of both strong and weak ties
- The opportunities you have found to grow your brand among people who care about who you are and how you can help them

Connect the Dots between Clients and Networking

When making the case for adding a networking habit, connect the dots between new business and networking initiatives. Review how networking has helped you to:

- Meet new people who became clients, colleagues, or friends
- Learn about new trends, ideas, issues that lead to greater excellence at work or to new work initiatives
- Develop a diverse set of resources to satisfy requests from colleagues, clients, and friends

The first place to document these successes is your new matter form. In addition to noting the source of the client and who is the originator, add context about the where, why, how, and by whom the "hire you" decision was made.

When you add the client to your contacts list or database enter not only how they heard about you but also interests you share with them, other people in your firm and network you want to introduce them to or events you want to invite them to. Consider hosting a seminar or dinner where you bring together a handful of clients and colleagues whom you think would be interested in knowing each other. Clients usually love these events, especially when they can share industry updates with contemporaries. Acting on these points makes you a connector, someone who offers value by knowing how to help other people.

When you host events for prospects and clients, you need to capture data on the entire process.

- Pre-event planning:
  - Purpose of event/definition of success
  - Guest selection criteria
  - Event specifics, including topic, speaker, networking opportunities, and so on.
  - Invitations: paper or email, number of reminders or save the date cards
- Event:
  - Attendance tracking
  - Qualitative assessment of event—did audience seem involved, interested, receptive to information?
  - Were there any "aha" moments?
  - Highlights of key conversations

- Post-event follow-up:
  - Thank you notes to attendees, notes to no-shows and important non-attendees
  - Update contacts list
  - Develop follow-up piece—blog, article, alert—to send to attendee list to reinforce the topic and your expertise

Did you ask attendees to fill out an evaluation sheet before they left as to the topic's relevance to them, what they liked most about the event, and any suggestions for improvements? If you shared the event with colleagues, you need to determine who is responsible for follow-up. Who thanks people for coming, touches base with those who signed up and did not attend, and notes those who remain missing-in-action? Who will draft a personal follow-up plan for the seminar guests you saw who were really interested?

Be sure to track all costs, both time and money, from the invitations through the event to the follow-up so that when you look back six months later you can compare costs to revenues from new clients or referrals.

Usually events are only one of many touch points along the path from stranger to client, but too often the steps are not recorded. You need metrics in order to attribute new work or new clients to a specific seminar, dinner, or knowledge exchange. If a networking connection enjoys many free opportunities at your expense but never becomes a client or referrer, you may want to figure out where the disconnect lies.

If detailed data collection seems overwhelming, go back to what is important and focus your efforts on two groups of clients:

- Your 80/20: the 20 percent [or less] of your clients who provide 80 percent of revenues
- The small handful of next-tier clients you want to cultivate into the top level

Or focus on your top prospects. You are then concentrating on your current primary revenue sources and your future revenue sources. Usually this brings your focus down to a manageable number of people.

Create a Habit

Q: Why should you want networking planning and implementation to become a habit?

A: So that it becomes routine: a regularly-scheduled time allotment in your day/week.

If you don't make measurement a regularly scheduled habit, you are less likely to do it. Once an activity is a habit, it is "in your base," just as ongoing expenditures are in a budget base as compared to one-time or extraordinary expenditures.

To make networking a habit, begin by reviewing your daily work pattern so that you can find a convenient time to slot these activities into your work life. Look for natural lulls in your workday or points of transition between activities. Transition points are natural places for amending your routine. Think about your workday pattern.

- Do you come to work early in order to plan your day before you become distracted by daily "fires"?
- Are you a slow starter? A morning person? A lunch at your desk but leave on the 5:15 p.m. train person?
- What are your biorhythms? Tired after lunch? Slow around 4 p.m.? A dawdler until your second cup of morning coffee?
- When do you take breaks—to get coffee, gossip with a colleague, go to the bathroom?

Identify the small gaps sprinkled throughout your workday that you can allot to marketing. In a 15-minute increment, you can:

- Skim the news for relevant trends that impact your world or your clients' worlds.
- Research people you plan to meet or have met.
- Check your LinkedIn news feed and connection updates.
- Contact ten people on LinkedIn—people to add to your contacts, contacts you've not touched base with in a while, contacts with whom you want to share information.
- Make a networking call or two.
- Plan next week's networking activities—where you will go, why you want to spend time on the activity, and what you will do there.
- Review and consider areas of success and areas you need to modify to be successful.

Identify the time of day you want to execute this habit and then calendar it. It is easier to use small chunks of time at specified times of the day or week rather than designate Friday afternoons for networking. Large time blocks tend to get whittled away by immediate crises.

The best networkers integrate networking into their daily lives. It is not a separate activity but rather part of who they are and what they do, related to their attitude of inquiry, continuous curiosity about the world around them, and a need to be useful to others.

Bonnie Hagen, COO of Bright Energy Services, says, "Networking is integrated into my life even when I attend activities at my kids' schools."

For Marc W. Halpert, LinkedIn trainer, networking is a "full-time job. I am always hustling, always marketing. Always looking for the psychic reward that comes from making good connections."

Keys to Effective Measurement and Evaluation

These measurements are primarily qualitative, but that doesn't mean data collection is unimportant. It is a complement to memory. Studies show that memories are not equivalent to photographs of past events. They more closely approximate impressionists' paintings. What is remembered is altered by the emotions surrounding the endeavor.

Tracking adds to memory with data that can be measured and counted, even if it is only ordinal numbers, such as seminar attendance. Over time, these data accumulate into patterns that can be evaluated to see whether you are moving toward your goals, targeting appropriate audiences, and creating beneficial linkages that lead to friendships, resources, and work.

Final Thoughts: Strategic Networking Needs to Reflect *You*

Begin with your mindset. How you approach networking activities will imprint everything you do. If you have a positive attitude, an inquiring mind, an interest in others and an ability to communicate the value of what you do to others, you will be successful.

If you view networking as a chore or as scary, difficult, and intimidating, your body language will reflect these feelings, making you seem inauthentic. Plan to create a safe space for yourself at networking events. Use writing and speaking skills to share your message with others in your network.

You know where you are comfortable. Go there. A friend of mine lives in Nevada but follows the University of Georgia football team. During football season she goes to a local bar every weekend to join other cheering and groaning Georgia fans. She knew no one when she went to the first game, but several games later she had become one of them. She doesn't know she is networking; she thinks she is just having fun.

There is no networking right or wrong. There is just authentic and inauthentic. If you know what you are looking for, you can find and meet appropriate people anywhere. Select networking venues that interest you. Let your curiosity lead you. You need to be interacting with sources of business in order to grow. Whether you are introvert, extrovert, or somewhere in-between, there is a networking setting that will work for you. Just find it.[1]

1. Go to Appendix 3, pages 217–218, to find out what the interviewees identified as networking likes and dislikes, and their suggestions for novice networkers.

People Interviewed and Networking Organizations Profiled

1

APPENDIX

Information on People Interviewed

Name	Title	Company	What s/he does[1]
David J. Abeshouse	Attorney	Law Office of David Abeshouse	Mediator and arbitrator, founder of the Attorney Roundtable[2]
Roger E. Barton	Managing partner	Barton LLP	Corporate lawyer
Bernadette Beekman	Managing Director	HireCounsel	Placement of temporary attorneys, lawyer
Jeffrey A. Blutstein	Owner	Financial Logistics	Financial advocate
Lenny Carraturo	Vice President, business development officer	Wells Fargo Bank	Middle Market Banking
Hollace Topol Cohen	Partner	Fisher Broyles	Bankruptcy lawyer
Stacey Cohen	President & CEO	Co-communications	Marketing Communications firm

1. Company and what s/he does are accurate as of the date they were interviewed. Some people are now in other positions.
2. Founders of networking groups profiled in the book. Many of the other interviewees have founded groups.

continued

Name	Title	Company	What s/he does[1]
Stacy Francis	President & CEO	Francis Financial	Financial planning & wealth management
Richard Friedman	Managing partner	Richard Friedman PLLC	Management side employment litigator
Marcia R. Golden	President	DJD Golden Advertising Inc.	Marketing and public relations
Amy B. Goldsmith	Partner	Tartar Krinsky & Drogin	Intellectual property lawyer
Karen Haas	Sales representative	Certa-Pro Paint	Salesperson
Bonnie Hagen	COO	Bright Energy Services	Salesperson
Marc W. Halpert	Owner	Connect2collaborate	LinkedIn trainer
Larry Hutcher	Co-managing partner	Davidoff Hutcher & Citron LLP	Litigator
Fred C. Klein	Senior partner	Klein Zelman Rothermel & Schess LLP	Employment [management side] lawyer, founder of Gotham networking group
Linda A. Klein	Senior managing shareholder	Baker Donelson	Corporate lawyer
Martin S. Klein	Partner	Kamerman, Uncyk, Soniker & Klein P.C.	T&E and tax lawyer
James K. Landau	Partner	McCarthy Fingar LLP	Litigator
Dan Lear	Director of industry relations	Avvo	Online legal marketplace marketing, lawyer
Andrew C. Peskoe	Senior partner & owner	Golenbock Eiseman Assor Bell & Peskoe, LLP	Corporate lawyer
Vikram Rajan	Co-founder	phoneBlogger.net	Ghost writer, blogs, newsletters

Name	Title	Company	What s/he does[1]
Abby Rosmarin	Mediator, conflict coach, lawyer	McCarthy Fingar LLP	Mediator, founder of Face-to-Face networking group
Jonathan Rosen	Founder	Collaberex	Lawyer, founder of Collaborex
David Rosenbaum	Principal	Citrin Cooperman	IT consultant, founder of WBN networking group
Alla Roytberg	Partner	Law Firm & Mediation Practice of Alla Roytberg, P.C.	Lawyer, mediator
Nancy Schess	Partner	Klein Zelman Rothermel & Schess LLP	Employment [management side] lawyer, founder of Gotham networking group
Marcia Sloman	President	Under Control Organizing	Professional organizer
Stephen M. Smith	President	Stephen M. Smith & Co.	CPA
Steven Spielvogel	Partner	Gallion & Spielvogel	Litigator, founder of the International Network of Boutique & Independent Law Firms [INBLF]
Armanda C. Squadrilli	Broker	Douglas Elliman Real Estate	Real estate broker
Ronald K. Stair	Principal & actuary	Creative Plan Design, Ltd.	Actuarial plan design consultant
Mark Taylor	Chair, speaker, cultural architect	Vistage	Master Chair of Vistage CEO groups in NYC
Jessica Thaler-Parker	Vice President	Financial Institution	Regulatory Change and Project Managment
Ellen Volpe	President	ABA American Business Associates [ABA]	Networking group owner and facilitator, American Business Associates

Networking Groups Profiled, by Chapter

Chapter 1

Group Profile: WESTCHESTER PROFESSIONALS: Face-to-Face

Chapter 5

BNI
Gotham City Networking, Inc.
Westchester Business Network [WBN]
American Business Associates [ABA]
The Attorney Roundtable [ART]
The International Network of Boutique & Independent Law Firms [INBLF]
Primerus
Vistage
Collaberex

Worksheets 2

APPENDIX

Chapter 2: Creating a Research-Based Action Plan

Worksheet 2.1 Personal Preferences: Work-Life Balance

1. Where do you want your career to be in five years?
   a. Where do you want to be at the end of your career?
2. Thinking about the rest of your life,
   a. How important is it to you to grow your business or practice?
      i. Very important
      ii. Important
      iii. Depends on other things in my life
      iv. Not very important
      v. Not important to me
   b. Why is this important or not to you?
   c. If growth is important, what investment of time and money is it worth to you?
      i. Time
      ii. Money

continued

3. Is your self-image rooted in your work?

4. How important is personal time to you compared to work time?

5. Do you like the environment of the place where you work?

    a. If so, what do you find pleasing about it?

    b. If not, why not, and what would you change?

6. Do you like where you live?

    a. If so, what do you find pleasing about it?

    b. If not, why not, and what would you change?

7. How would you define a perfect work-life balance?

Worksheet 2.2 Your Work

1. What kind of work do you do?
2. What do you like best about your work?[1]
    a. Describe a specific example of work you enjoyed.
    b. Describe an instance in which you were proud of the results obtained.
3. What is the most profitable part of your practice?
4. What is the long-term outlook for growth in your practice area?
5. What does your client base look like now?
    a. How would you define your best clients?[2]
        i. What are the characteristics of your best clients?[3]
        ii. Do you want to continue to work with this type of client?
            1. If not, what kinds of clients do you want?
    b. What are the names of the clients in your 80/20%?[4]
        i. Names
        ii. Are their characteristics the same as those of your best clients?
            1. List any different characteristics here.
6. If you could change some things about the work you do, what would those changes look like?
    a. Are you likely to move in this direction?
        i. If so, when?
        ii. If not, why not?

1. E.g., fact-finding, research, devising a solution for your client, counseling clients, winning, working with other team members, etc.
2. E.g., famous, important issues or problems, revenue producers, large, dominant in their field, etc.
3. E.g., Company characteristics include: type of business, size, industry, growth position of business, work you do for them, number of years as a client, potential for additional work. Individuals' characteristics include where they live, living arrangements, family relationships, economic level, cultural and/or religious beliefs, their personalities, etc.
4. 80%/20% refers to the 20% of your clients who account for 80% of your revenue.

Worksheet 2.3 Assets and Liabilities of the Company/Firm You Work For

1. Entity name and name of your place of work if it is a subpart of the business
2. Company/firm size:
   a. Number of offices
   b. Number of professionals:
      i. Total
      ii. In your office
      iii. In your practice area
   c. Geographic span:
      i. Local—one geographic location
      ii. Multistate
      iii. International
   d. Size of the office you are in compared to competitors in your location:
      i. Large
      ii. Medium
      iii. Small
3. Services/products offered: If you are in a professional service firm, list the major practice areas and prioritize them according to their size and contribution to revenue. If you work for a business, identify the major product lines/areas of business.
4. How would you define the essence of your employer's brand?
5. What are the firm's "80/20" clients' characteristics
6. Who are your employer's major competitors that could impact your own marketing efforts?
7. How can the firm, its reputation, and resources help you meet your goals? Be as precise as possible.
8. Will the characteristics or clientele of the firm present obstacles you need to overcome to meet your goals? Be as precise as possible.

Worksheet 2.4 Social Interaction Preferences

1. How much do you care about other people and their issues?
   a. Are you curious about their opinions, their life choices and personal choices?
   b. How interested are you in helping other people achieve their goals?
2. Do you like sharing personal or work-related stories with other people?
3. Do you consider yourself to be more of an extrovert or an introvert?
   a. Would you rather read a book or hang out with friends?
   b. Do you prefer solo recreational activities or team sports?
4. What networking activities do you like to do?
5. What networking activities do you dislike doing?
6. How willing are you to try new networking activities until you find one that works well for you?

Worksheet 2.5 SWOT Analysis

Strengths[1]	Opportunities[2]
Weaknesses[1]	Threats[2]

1. Strengths and weaknesses refer to you in the context of the questions answered in Worksheets 2.1 through 2.4.
2. Opportunities and threats deal with phenoma in the external environment.

When you think about your goals give yourself a 12–18-month time frame. Because you may be too ambitious, write them down in order of priority so if you do not get to goal 3 you will still have made solid progress.

Worksheet 2.6 Goal Setting

Goal 1 Define

Estimated time frame:

Estimated money costs:

Why is this goal important to you?

How will you know when you have achieved this goal?

Goal 2 Define

Estimated time frame:

Estimated money costs:

Why is this goal important to you?

How will you know when you have achieved this goal?

Goal 3 Define

Estimated time frame:

Estimated money costs:

Why is this goal important to you?

How will you know when you have achieved this goal?

Worksheet 2.7 Marketing Action Plan

For each goal, develop one or two strategies. For each strategy, devise one or two tactics, i.e., techniques to implement the strategies.

Goal 1 Write in goal 1 from Worksheet 2.6.

Two strategies

Strategy 1:

Tactic 1:

Tactic 2:

Strategy 2:

Tactic 1:

Tactic 2:

Goal 2 Write in goal 2 from Worksheet 2.6.

Two strategies

Strategy 1:

Tactic 1:

Tactic 2:

Strategy 2:

Tactic 1:

Tactic 2:

Goal 3 Write in goal 3 from Worksheet 2.6.

Two strategies

Strategy 1:

Tactic 1:

Tactic 2:

Strategy 2:

Tactic 1:

Tactic 2:

Chapter 3: Who's in Your Network?

Worksheet 3.1 Creating a Top Contacts Group

Person's name, contact information	What person does, Company's industry or individual's demographic	How you met the person? How well you know the person	What is the basis of your close connection with the person?	How can you help this person?	How can this person help you?	Where/how will you connect with this person?	How do you define a successful relationship with this person?
Add more rows as needed							

Chapter 8: Preparations for Strategic Conversations

Table 8.1 80/20 clients

Client name	**Industry/SIC or NAICS #[7]**	**Number of years as a client**	**Services used and services *client* could use**	**Factors influencing ability to get additional work**
Client #1				
Client #2				
Client #3				
Add more rows as needed				

7. SIC stands for Standard Industrial Classification, NAICS stands for the North American Industry Classification System, "[which] is the standard used by Federal statistical agencies in classifying business establishments for the purpose of collecting, analyzing, and publishing statistical data related to the U.S. business economy." Home page at https://www.census.gov/eos/www/naics/.

Worksheet 8.1 Characteristics of Your Target Persona

What is her/his name?
What does s/he look like? [Find a picture that looks like this person]
How old?
How educated?
Where does s/he work and live?
What are his/her living arrangements?
Who is in his/her family and what role do they play in his/her life?
Who are the key influencers in the persona's life?
How do they influence his/her buying decisions?

What motivates this persona?
What are his/her interests outside of work?
What hobbies or outside interests does the personna have?
How do these interests impact how s/he interacts with the world around him/her?
How does s/he feel about major societal forces such as politics, religious, or gender discrimination?
What are his/her hot buttons?
What makes the persona happy?
Is s/he a penny pincher or a spendthrift?
Does s/he have a personal budget?
How does s/he prefer to pay for purchases?
Where does s/he go for information related to purchases?
What social media platforms does s/he participate on?
Does s/he tend to be a lurker, commentator, or creator on social media?

Who does s/he work for?
What does his/her employer do? What specific services/products does the firm/company sell?
What does s/he do for a living?
What is his/her title at work?
What does s/he do during an average workday?
What are her/his key responsibilities and challenges?
What kind of rewards and frustrations are related to his/her work?
Does s/he make or influence buying decisions?
How important is his/her job to his/her identity?
How much money does s/he make?

What media does s/he go to for information?
What communication devices does s/he prefer to use?

Does s/he read physical books or magazines or newspapers, or does she prefer digital media options?
How does s/he want to be contacted?

What are his/her current needs?
What can you do to meet those needs?
How will you communicate to her/him your ability to help him/her?

Worksheet 8.2 Features/Benefits Comparison

Your attributes	Features of your practice	Benefits of these activities for the target	Relationship to the target's wants, needs, and desires
What you do			
Why you do it			
What you know			
Your approach to client service			

Worksheet 8.3 Elevator Speech Components

30-second basics:

My name is ______________________.

I am a ______[kind of professional]______ who works with ____[your niche]/[your kind of clients]____.

I love what I do, because I create ______[work product]______ to help my clients avoid problems such as ______________________.

OR

I help my clients be successful by taking advantage of opportunities such as ______________________ by __________[what you do]__________.

OR

I really enjoy helping clients ______[results – financial or physical or emotional]______.

I would welcome a chance to ________[what you want as a next step]________.

Again, my name is ________________ and my company is ________________.

Additional components

Persuasive statements about your capabilities

- Quantitative, impactful statistics:
  - Marketplace share
  - Number of key players in the niche you work with
  - Number of years' experience for you/your group
  - Size/resources/expertise of your group compared to your competition
  - Number of cases won/deals done [whatever s publicly available]
- Qualitative descriptors:
  - Approach to client service
  - Transparency of the process
  - Likeability—you and your team
    - Enthusiasm is as important as expertise
    - Personal connections between you and your team and their team
  - Understanding of how the client feels about the situation
  - Ability to empathize and validate
  - Understanding of the full context of the problem—all relevant aspects of the problem as compared to just those that are germane to the specific matter
  - Value of what you do for your clients
    - Case studies/stories

What makes you different

- Approach to specific problems/issues
- What you do better than your competitors
- Experience with your target client's specific problems/issues
- Knowledge relevant to the issues/players

- Proprietary products
- Location(s)
- Credentials
- Expertise, e.g., your legal knowledge or your knowledge of the tax code or your knowledge of available financial wealth instruments
- Personal qualities, including enthusiasm, energy, passion
- Availability/chemistry
- Cost

Benefits of what you do

- Produce results:
  - Take advantage of an opportunity
  - Save or make money for the client
  - Help clients to grow
  - Reverse a wrong
  - Enforce rights
  - Apportion assets
- Minimize risk:
  - Prevent a complication
  - Circumvent an obstacle
  - Predictable costs
  - Time and money savings
- Reduce emotional costs for the individual who is the client:
  - Issues of safety
  - Control
  - Financial security
  - Future impact

Chapter 10: The Three-Part Networking Implementation Strategy

Worksheet 10.1 Pre- and Post-Activity Worksheet

Event ____

Date ________________ Time ____________________

Time set aside for event preparation [date and time of day] ____________________

Type of event: ________ one-on-one ________ group event

If a group, what is the name of the sponsoring group? ____________________

Are you a member of the group? _____ yes _____ no

Are you _____ going alone ______with others _______ meeting others there

Pre-Event

Reasons I want to attend this networking opportunity:

____

____

____

My goal: ____

____

People I plan to contact before the event and why: ____________________

____

____

Conversation points

Tweaks to my elevator pitch and value proposition: ____________________

____

____

____

____

People I would like to meet or reconnect with: ____________________

____

Post-Event

How did you feel about the event at the end?

____ enjoyed it more than I thought I would

____ enjoyed it

____ enjoyed it less than I anticipated

Why?____

____

____

How much of your pre-planning was useful at the event?

____ all of it ____ most of it ____ none of it

Why?____

____

____

Did I meet my goal? _____ yes _____ no

Why did this result happen? ________________________________

____

____

What are my next steps? Did I schedule next steps? ________________

____

____

____

____

Is there anything I want to do differently next time? ________________

____

____

____

Time

Time spent in pre-activity preparation ______________________________

Research ______________________________

Reaching out to specific people ______________________________

Outreach to general audiences ______________________________

Agenda building ______________________________

Transportation mode/time spent ______________________________

Event ______________________________

Time spent doing follow-up ______________________________

Categorization, planning next steps______________________________

Notes______________________________

Total time ______________________________

Resources Used

Help from others [be specific] ______________________________

Money ______________________________

Did the activity meet my expectations?

Surpassed expectations _____

Met expectations _____

Below expectations _____

Disaster _____

Summary [actions, feelings, happenings, etc.] ______________________________

____

____

____

____

Chapter 11: The Art of Giving and Getting Referrals

Worksheet 11.1 Referral Strategies Worksheet

Your goals for 20__ ______________________________

____

____

What kind of referrals are you looking for? ______________________________

____

____

What kind of people do you want to be referred to? ______________________________

____

____

Names of possible referrers

Colleagues in your profession: ______________________________

Colleagues in complementary businesses: ______________________________

Colleagues who also service your key client(s): ______________________________

Colleagues who target the same market as you: ______________________________

Clients: ______________________________

Employees: ______________________________

Family/friends: ______________________________

Academic connections: ______________________________

Strategic partners: ______________________________

Strategic thinkers: ______________________________

What can you do for them?

____

____

How can you add value to their relationships with their clients?

____

____

____

How can you help them in terms of visibility and marketing?

____

____

____

How can you help them build their business?

____

____

____

What will your elevator pitch and value proposition be when speaking to referrers?

____

____

____

How will you make your message relevant to them?

____

____

What is your "touches" plan to stay top of mind with your best referral sources?

____

____

____

How will you combine online and in-person activities so they build on one another?

____

____

____

What kind of sharing, reinforcing communities can you build? With which referral categories?

____

____

____

What will success look like for you?

____

____

____

What tools will you use to measure results?

____

____

____

Chapter 12: Putting It All Together: Integrating, Evaluating, and Measuring Activities

Worksheet 12.1 Networking Evaluation Report

Organization/ activity	Purpose of group/activity	Time spent	Money spent	Results*	Additional comments

*1–5 scale [5 = exceeded expectations, 1 = failed]

Additional Insights

3

APPENDIX

Chapter 1: Strategic Networking Explained

Abby Rosmarin Groups from her Website: https://www.rosmarincoaching.com/abbys-why (December 2018)

Mediation + ADR Affiliations

Mediation Counsel, McCarthy Fingar, LLP

Executive Director, NY Association of Collaborative Professionals

Member, Mediation Roster, Supreme Court of New York, Commercial Division, Westchester County

Member, Westchester Supreme Court Matrimonial Mediation Roster

Certified Mediator, Westchester Mediation Center, Cluster, Inc.

Divorce Mediator, New York Peace Institute

Member, Part 137 Panel of Arbitrators and Mediators, Joint Committee on Fee Disputes and Conciliation

Member (past), NYC Family Court Mediation Panel

Mental Health

NYS Licensed Mental Health Counselor

Parenting Coordinator

Onsite provider of mental health services for employees of a privately held company

Collaborative divorce team member

Mental Health Counselor, Family Services of Westchester

Mental Health Counselor, permitee, Concordia College

Certified Facilitator and Administrator, Strength Deployment Inventory, Portrait of Personal Strength and Portrait of Overdone Strengths Assessments

Facilitator, Youth and Police Initiative, North American Family Institute

Trained Coach, Money Harmony

Legal
Assistant General Counsel, Peugeot Motors of America

NYS Certified Guardian, Court Evaluator and Attorney for Alleged Incapacitated Persons

Crosby, Heafey, Roach & May; Rosenman & Colin

Member, State Bars, NY and California

Group Facilitation
Pivotal Moments

Divorce Support Group, 92nd Street Y

Spousal Loss Support Group, Bereavement Center of Westchester

Affiliations
Manhattanville College School of Business, Adjunct Faculty Member,

FamilyKind, Advisory Council

Gilda's Club Westchester, Program Task Force

Westchester Women's Bar Association, Co-chair Mediation Committee

New York Center for Law and Justice, Board Member, Northern Westchester Hospital, community member

Ethics Committee, Patient & Family Partnership Council (works with the Hospital's leadership and professional staff to optimize patient-centered care), Credentials Committee (granting of hospital privileges), Performance Improvement Coordinating Group (examines quality and patient safety processes- past participation)

NY Association of Collaborative Professionals

Academy of Professional Family Mediators, Founding Member

WEDC Senior Providers Network

Orion Resource Group (Elder Care), Westchester Chapter Leader (past)

National Counseling Association

Association of Conflict Resolution, Elder Decision-making and Conflict Resolution Section

Family and Divorce Mediation Council of Greater New York

New York State Council Divorce Mediation

New York Society of Association Executives, Executive Women in Nonprofits SIG

Committee on Special Education, Parent member (past)

Stacy Francis' Current Memberships

From the Francis Financial website, https://francisfinancial.com/team/stacy-francis-2/ and the personal interview.

General Mixed Membership Group
BNI Chapter, Manhattan 12—The Flagship Chapter, chair

Target Market Group
The Association of Divorce Financial Planners' (ADFP) Greater New York Metro Chapter, co-director

Honorary Groups
The Women Presidents' Organization (WPO)

The Private Risk Management Association (PRMA), honoree member

CNBC's Digital Financial Advisor Council

Professional Associations
The National Association of Personal Financial Advisors (NAPFA), director

The Financial Planning Association (FPA), director

Nonprofit Board
Savvy Ladies, a nonprofit organization founded by Stacy to educate and empower women to take control of their finances, founder and chair

Chapter 2: Creating a Research-Based Action Plan

List of Possible Tactics

Knowledge Sharing/Thought Leadership Tactics

- Speeches
- Articles
    - Industry or issue-specific publications
    - Local publications
    - Online publications
- Blogs
- Newsletters
- Specific issue alerts
- White papers
- Books
- Your website

Visibility Tactics

- Public relations—media stories and quotes
- Advertising
- Organization publications
- Charity ads
- An active presence on LinkedIn, Facebook, and similar broad-based sites
- Your presence at online sites used by and valued by your target market
- Online key word advertising
- Organization participation
  - Board of directors
  - Program participation
  - Sponsorships
- Your website
- Volunteer activities

Promotional Tactics to Make It Easier to Find You

- Advertising
  - Print or online media
  - Nonprofit and gala event journals
  - Event sponsorships
- Business cards
- Your website
- Directories: online and print
- Brochures
- Cards
  - Birthday
  - Holiday
  - Anniversary of a positive decision for a client
- Gifts

Common Personal Networking Activities

Group memberships

- Join groups that help you reach your goals
- Attend meetings
- Participate on committees
- Hold leadership positions

Personal activities

- Writing
  - Articles
  - Client alerts
  - Blogs
  - White papers
  - Responses to online discussions
- Speaking
  - At firm-sponsored events
  - At conferences
  - For education credit

- Meeting attendance
  - Networking group meetings
  - Other group meetings
  - Continuing education
  - Conferences
  - Family and community events [e.g., little league games, PTA nights, church, birthdays, etc.]
- Meetings one-on-one or in small groups
  - Coffee
  - Meals
  - Go together to meetings, conferences, events

Work-sponsored events

- "Meet and Greet" get-togethers
- Seminars
- Events

Chapter 7: Online Networking Venues

Helpful Hints for Online Networking

Continue your in-person networking strategy online:

- Remember what your goals are.
- Remember the characteristics of your target persona and go where they go.
- Think where your ideal referrer is likely to go and follow them.
- Make a list of the topics you want to learn more about.
- Join the same groups as the aspirational people you follow on LinkedIn.
- Participate in group discussions, adding value with shared materials or your contribution to an ongoing dialogue.

Courtesy first—thank people:

- When they connect with you
- When they look at your profile
- When they like, share, or comment on your posts

Keep growing your online connections:

- Add people you meet at in-person events.
- Review friends' and colleagues' connections and request introduction.
- Review profiles of people who view your profile and seek connections when appropriate.
- When you see synergy, make introductions.
- Search through your various schools and previous employer names to link with old friends.
- Look through the membership of your LinkedIn groups for connections.

Give to get:

- Endorse your connections' skills and expertise.

- Share colleagues' content with your connections.
- Write testimonials praising people you collaborate with or people who help you.
- Make friendly online introductions by adding a bit about each person and saying why you think it will be a good connection for each of them.

Keep all posts on all venues professional:

- That photo of you on the beach that you posted ten years ago is still available online. Think if it presents the image you want to present today. If it doesn't take it down.
- Remember social media, like in-person events, has a social component—so emphasize sharing rather than selling.
- Google yourself monthly to be sure your reputation remains intact.

Chapter 10: The Three-Part Networking Implementation Strategy

Intangible Best Practices

Consider your image and dress for the event—be appropriately fashionable.

Set your body language to optimistic and confident.

Look people in the eye when you meet them, smile and give a firm handshake.

Be approachable and authentic.

Use your knowledge of body language to project a confident, positive attitude.

Focus on *only one* person at a time.

Ask personal, memorable questions.

Practice active listening to key in on the intent behind the words.

Let people see and experience your accessibility.

Have an upbeat, open attitude.

Look forward to learning more about those in the room with you.

Relax and let conversations happen.

Get in the mood—if you think you will have a good time, you probably will.

Networking Event Best Practices

Act like a host. Welcome people with a firm handshake, a direct regard, and a real smile.

Remember that networking is a two-way street and always try to help others.

Embody a positive attitude when you talk about your work. Show pride and enthusiasm for your work skills and work product and respect for your clients.

Prefer to be interested rather than interesting.

Maintain eye contact when talking to people by focusing on them and their conversation so they feel special and heard. Don't let your eyes wander around the room.

Listen. Ask. Watch. Use all your senses to understand as much as you can about each person you meet.

In any conversation, the person who talks the most thinks it was a brilliant interaction.

If you make a faux pas [forget a name, spill a drink] use humor and a laugh to clear the air.

Wear your name tag on your right lapel so people can see it when they shake your hand.

Don't go to events hungry or thirsty. Eat and drink in moderation.

Don't post unprofessional photos of the event on your online accounts. Nothing on the Internet is private. Everything on the Internet remains there, and findable, forever.

Be polite, courteous, thoughtful, and positive.

Ask for a copy of the attendee list.

Seek out the person who planned the event or was in charge of the program and thank them.

Make sure to fulfill any promises you made as soon as possible.

Have fun.

Conversation One-Liners[1]

Conversation one-liners to begin a conversation:
Walk up to strangers; introduce yourself to people standing alone.

- "I don't know anyone here and you seem to be alone so I thought I would begin to know people by introducing myself to you." Or,
- "Hello. I saw you standing alone and thought two of us might be better than one. My name is ___________." Or,
- "I don't know anyone here and since you are standing alone I thought you might be a new member too, so I decided to come over and introduce myself."
- To signify your interest in the person you are talking to, comment on some aspect of their clothing—unusual jewelry, lovely color, etc.

Walk up to people you haven't seen in a long time.

- "Hi ___, what's new with you?"
- "It's been a long time since I last saw you. What's the most exciting thing you've done since we last spoke?"

When introducing people add a bit about each person [business or personal] to get their conversation off to a good start.

1. Adapted from conversations with interviewees.

Joining a group of two or more:

- "You look like you are having an interesting conversation, may I listen in?"

Conversation one-liners to leave a conversation:

- "Please excuse me. I've enjoyed talking to you." or "It was nice meeting you."
- "Please excuse me. I promised to spend some time with ________ and I see s/he just walked in."
- "I've enjoyed our conversation, but I set a goal of meeting three people tonight, and I still have two to go."
- "I don't want to monopolize your time. Let's plan to get together. I'll call you next week."
- The usual drink refill, phone call, work email or bathroom break.

Conversation Ice Breakers[2]

About the event:

- "Have you ever heard this speaker before?"
- "Why did you decide to come to this meeting?"
- "Are you a member of this group?" "Why did you join?"
- "I came because I want to learn more about [the topic]."
- "This reminds me of college mixers. In those days I always waited for the white knight who would save me, so when I saw you standing here, I thought I would come over to be a white knight for you."

About yourself vis-a-vis the person you are talking to:

- "Hello. My name is ___________. I help people __ [focus on an aspect of what you do that is relevant to the people you are meeting] ___________."
- "I have been looking forward to meeting you because [something you share in common—a person, hobby, client, work interests, etc.] ________. "
    - The five most important words in professional services networking: "How can I help you?"
    - "Who can I introduce you to?"
    - "Is there anyone here you would like to meet?"

Join a food or beverage line:

- Ask a question about the food or drink.
- Ask event-related questions [see above].

Join a group of people at a pause in their conversation:

- "You look like you are having an interesting conversation, may I listen in?"
- "Could I give up my wall flower status and join your group?"

Networking Negatives and Corrections[3]

Don't let negative thoughts or a bad mood sideline you. If you expect to have a lousy time, you will. Instead do whatever works to put you in a convivial mood.

---

2. Adapted from conversations with interviewees.
3. Adapted from conversations with interviewees.

Don't explain who you are with a plain "I am a lawyer or financial planner or accountant." Instead, embellish with more about your professional focus, values, and/or the benefits you provide for clients.

Don't focus on quantity business card collections. Instead spend quality time talking to potentially significant relationships.

Don't pig out on either the food or liquor. Instead remember that your purpose is win-win conversations, which can't happen if your mouth is full or your brain is fuzzy. Some people make a point of eating a snack before any networking meeting even if it includes a meal.

Don't spend the time sitting and waiting for people to drop by like a spider in a spider web. Mingle.

Don't sell. Invite awareness of what you do through stories that link your skill set to your audience's needs and interests

Don't be a taker. Use your knowledge and resources to help others.

By showcasing what you do to people who could use your services, you create many potential clients and referral sources.

Chapter 11: The Art of Giving and Getting Referrals

Referral Relationship Sins

Sins of the Referrer:

- Doesn't return phone calls or email requests for help
- Throws out possible introductions without offering to grease the way
- Is arrogant or stand-offish when asked for help
- Offers introductions and then fails to follow through
- Takes his/her contacts pool for granted
- Has a weak contacts list

Sins of the Referred:

- Boring—lack a memorable story about their competencies
- Lacks sufficient practice area expertise/experience
- Overpromises, under-delivers
- Oversteps boundaries set by the referrer or the referred-to
- Doesn't keep the others informed of progress
- Takes referrers and referrals for granted

Sins of the Referred-to:

- Doesn't follow through on the introduction request
- Forgets to thank the referrer
- Doesn't offer feedback as to the appropriateness or inappropriateness of the referred
- Doesn't let the referrer know when the engagement is completed

Two Real Examples of Referral Value from Connectors in My Gotham City Networking Group

Gotham City Networking Group has a listserv for its members that is used to make requests, send thanks for requests answered, and remind members of Gotham events and opportunities. These are two real emails culled from 2017 listserv traffic, edited a bit for clarity and to preserve anonymity. [Emails are Condensed]

Email 1

Subject Line: AB and CD and Gotham—All Strike Again

"For many of us the value Gotham brings are referrals into our businesses. But if that is the only value you get from Gotham you are missing out. Gotham can also make you look brilliant to your existing clients. . . . "Recently I put out calls for help for a client that suffered a devastating fire.

"First call [which was for a title search on the property was answered by [an insurance agent] who got us the documents we needed amazingly fast.

"Second call for a contact at Chase Bank was answered by a lobbyist [who] navigated a bank bureaucracy in record time.

"And what is the result of both? The mortgage [which was paid to a small community bank years ago] was released in a matter of days.

"And by the way they were not the only ones to answer the calls for help. . . . please accept my heartfelt thanks."

Email 2

Answer to a request for help with a tricky mortgage refinancing issue.

"I suggest you speak with AK. If he can't help you I have a high-end attorney . . . that I can introduce you to, and if he can't help I have a mortgage broker who does a lot of out of the box financing deals. Let me know how far you want me to go—just contact info, e-introduces, ..."

Chapter 12: Putting It All Together: Integrating, Evaluating, and Measuring Activities

Interviewees' Opinions

The content of this book owes an extraordinary debt of gratitude to the expert networkers and connectors who took the time to share their insights with me. My final questions were: What do you like best and least about networking? What advice would you give those still on the fence?

Here are their answers.[4]

4. I combined similar answers into one phrase to eliminate redundancies.

Interviewees' Networking Likes

Making friends

Knowing people everywhere

High quality contacts

Playing the "match game" —matching people and needs

One-on-one networking because you can share what is in your heart

One-on-ones, which is where relationships are built

Meeting interesting people

Learning from others

Giving/helping others

Playing golf surrounded by people whose company you enjoy

Getting out of the office to be with other people

Hearing other peoples' stories

Getting "into a bubble" with other people

Going to events where you are welcomed by people you know

The sense of accomplishment after a successful meeting

Interviewees' Networking Dislikes

Takers/people who only want something for themselves

Salespeople

Bullshit

Promises made but not delivered

Disingenuous people

Insincere people

Lack of follow-up after a referral

Insufficient time to follow up

Throwaway connections

Networking can be a "time suck"

The need to "kiss a lot of frogs"

Walking into a room full of strangers

Cocktail parties

Boring meetings

Interviewees' Advice to Novice Networkers

Networking is essential, because if you hide no one will know where to find you.

Begin with a plan and know your key messages.

Don't try to fit a round peg in a square hole.

Follow your passions.

Be comfortable with who you are.

Add an activity outside your comfort zone and spend the time necessary to grow into it.

Get comfortable with your referral sources.

Find people to be with who you like and think are good networkers; copy their strong attributes.

Pick an area of interest and dig into it.

Call someone every day.

Be super curious.

Be persistent.

Be sincere.

Be genuine, friendly, warm.

Always be nice—everything I need to know I learned in kindergarten.

Only have an opinion about things that really matter to you.

Know your own strengths.

Learn from a mentor.

Get started.

Do it.

Get out there.

Index

W

X

Y